POPULAR

SHRUBS &
PERENNIALS

POPULAR

SHRUBS & PERENNIALS

An A-Z guide to low-maintenance plants

FRASER STEWART

This edition published by
Fraser Stewart Book Wholesale Ltd
Abbey Chambers
4 Highbridge Street
Waltham Abbey
Essex EN9 1DQ

Produced by Marshall Cavendish Books, London
(A division of Marshall Cavendish Partworks Ltd)

ISBN 1 85435 824 3
Printed and bound in Malaysia

Some of this material has previously appeared in
the Marshall Cavendish partwork *MY GARDEN*

CONTENTS

INTRODUCTION

Each profile is packed with information to help you select, buy
and successfully grow a wide range of popular and easily
available plants, from bright annuals to sturdy shrubs, and from
tiny alpines and rockery plants to climbers and trees.

**The Latin 'genus' or group
name to which plant species
belong**

Common name, if any, by
which genus or species is popularly
known

Clear colour photograph
of the most widespread
species

Illustration showing
average height and spread

**Description of general
characteristics,** such
as whether plants are
annuals, perennials,
shrubs or climbers

At-a-glance symbols that
focus on important
details

Colour photographs
illustrating other
popular species or,
where applicable,
fruits, blossoms or
autumn leaf colour

Information on where,
when and how to cultivate
and take care of your plants,
plus a number of recommended
varieties

Tips and hints on all
manner of things – from
growing and pruning to
drying and displaying

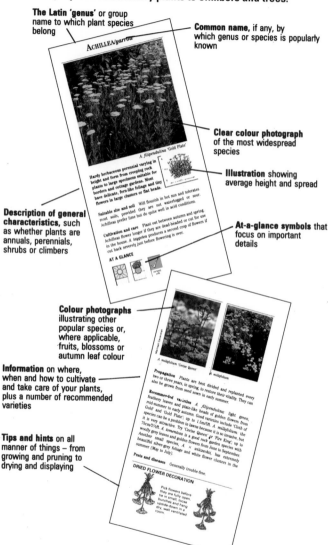

Use the information contained in the profiles to choose the right plants for
your garden and, once chosen, to aid you in planting and aftercare. The
book is a handy size – take it with you when you go shopping.

A. grandiflora

An attractive group of semi-evergreen
and deciduous shrubs. Medium sized,
with graceful, arching branches and
dainty trumpet-like flowers, they have a
long flowering season. Use in a
shrubbery or as a specimen plant.

Suitable site and soil Given the right conditions, they thrive
in most ordinary, well-drained soils and will also tolerate lime.
They need full sun to flower well. Plant them near a wall, if
possible, to give protection from harsh cold and winds.

Cultivation and care Plant out in April or October. Pruning
is not regularly required but, when necessary, cut back in
spring.

AT A GLANCE

LOVES FULL SUN   EASY TO GROW   DECIDUOUS   LOVES ALL SOIL

A. triflora

A. schumannii

Blooms appear on two to three-year-old wood, so pruning may reduce the number of flowers produced in the following year.

Propagation Long, outer shoots can be layered in the spring. To root cuttings, which should be 10–15cm/4–6in and semi-mature, taken in summer, you will need a cold frame or a propagator with bottom heat.

Recommended varieties *A. floribunda:* tender, semi-evergreen shrub up to 1.5m/5ft tall. Shiny green leaves and rosy red flowers throughout summer. *A. × grandiflora:* one of the hardiest and best, with dark, shiny green leaves and pink and white flowers from July to September; up to 1.8m/6ft tall. *A. schumannii:* smaller, semi-deciduous shrub with large, rosy lilac flowers from summer to autumn; up to 1.5m/5ft tall. *A. triflora:* one of the largest and hardiest, producing fragrant white flowers flushed with pink in early summer; up to 4.5m/15ft.

CUTTING BACK UNTIDY STEMS

Pruning encourages new growth. Cut out a few older shoots; shorten leggy growths.

A. koreana

Evergreen conifers, ranging from immensely tall forest trees to slow growing, compact species suitable for the average garden. Neat, symmetrical outlines and silvery foliage. Cones range in colour from green to purple.

4·6 m

3m

Suitable site and soil   Will grow in most soils except the very alkaline. Avoid exposed situations.

Cultivation and care   Feed lightly with a balanced fertilizer when growth starts, and keep the roots moist. The plant should have a single leading shoot, so prune competing side shoots to maintain a neat shape.

AT A GLANCE

LOVES DAMP SOIL

EVERGREEN

A. balsamea 'Hudsonia'

A. balsamea 'Nana'

Propagation   Sow seed in pots or seed boxes in a cold frame in autumn. Prick out when large enough. Plant out in spring, when about 30cm/12in high.

Recommended varieties   *A. koreana* (Korean fir): grows slowly to 4.6m/15ft; hardy and compact; bears purple cones, even as a young plant, following striking red, pink and green flowers. *A. balsamea* 'Hudsonia': dwarf 'mountain' form that gives a strong smell of balsam. *A. concolor* 'Glauca Compacta': dwarf silver fir; grows very slowly to 2m/6½ft. *A. homolepis* (Nikko fir): pale green leaves with white band; young cones are purple; bark flakes off, leaving red underbark.

Pests and diseases   Adelgids (similar to aphids) may suck sap from leaves in summer, causing distortion. Their waxy wool-like protective covering makes spraying ineffective. Fungal infection on young growth may cause 'die back'.

USING WOOD BARK TO HELP RETAIN WATER

To ensure that the roots of a newly planted fir are not disturbed, and to help water retention, apply a light mulch of pulverized wood bark, all around the plant. Water dry soil before mulching, and spread the bark to a depth of 6–7 cm.

A. microphylla

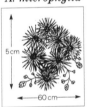

Dwarf, spreading evergreen plant with attractive, dense foliage and spiky red or purplish burrs. Most are long-lived, vigorous carpeters, too invasive for rock gardens but excellent as ground cover and useful for filling in gaps between paving stones in a patio or path.

Suitable site and soil   Open, sunny location in a sandy, well-drained soil. Although they will tolerate partial shade, plants may become thin and straggly.

Cultivation and care   Plant any time between early autumn and spring. Never let these plants become waterlogged or they will die. Can be invasive, so keep in check.

AT A GLANCE

A. *buchananii*

A. 'Blue Haze'

Propagation By division in spring or autumn, or by cuttings taken in summer. Most can be grown quite easily from seed.

Recommended varieties *A. microphylla:* bronze leaves; crimson burrs in autumn and early winter; only 5cm/2in high. *A.* 'Blue Haze': blue-green leaves, reddish brown burrs and red stems; height 10cm/4in, spread 60cm/2ft. *A. adscendens:* bronze leaves, and inconspicuous purple flowers in summer. *A. buchananii:* silver-grey foliage; red burrs in late summer. This variety is particularly good for growing in the cracks between paving stones. *A. novae-zelandiae:* good ground cover with long, adventurous stems and silky, hairy foliage. Attractive dark red spiky burrs in autumn. This species, known as New Zealand burr, is the most vigorous.

Pests and diseases Generally trouble-free.

SPECIAL EFFECTS WITH PAVING STONES

Acaena makes an effective and attractively coloured ground cover around a specimen shrub in a paved area of the garden. Remove a single paving slab to create a square planting area for a dwarf shrub such as *Thuja orientalis*.

A. mollis

Hardy herbaceous perennial with deeply cut leaves and tall spikes of purple or white flowers. A superb specimen plant, it should be grown where its fine, sculptural qualities can be fully appreciated.

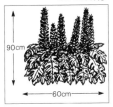

Suitable site and soil   Mild, sheltered locations and moist, well-drained soils. They will also tolerate a certain amount of shade, as long as the soil is not waterlogged.

Cultivation and care   Plant between autumn and spring. After flowering, cut stems level to the ground. In cold districts, for the first two winters protect the crowns, from which new shoots will eventually grow.

AT A GLANCE

A. mollis

A. spinosus

Propagation   By division in autumn or early spring. Alternatively, sow seed in spring. Pot up seedlings individually, harden off in mid-summer, then plant out in autumn. Root cuttings, 8cm/3in, can be taken in winter, potted individually once new growth appears, then treated as for seedlings.

Recommended varieties   *A. mollis:* bold, glossy grey-green leaves and hooded flowers of white, purple and green that bloom all summer. One of the finest focal plants at 90cm/3ft tall. *A. longifolius:* dark green, deeply cut leaves and long spikes of lilac flowers appearing from early to mid-summer; 75cm/2½ft tall. *A. spinosus:* very prickly, deeply divided, glossy green leaves and purple, white and green flowers from July to early September; height to 1.2m/4ft.

Pests and diseases   Generally trouble-free, but slugs can be a nuisance.

KEEP SLUGS AND SNAILS AT BAY

Protect a young acanthus plant by surrounding the plant with slug pellets or covering with a cloche – use the top from a large plastic bottle.

ACER/*maple*

A. drummondii 'Variegata'

Hardy deciduous trees or shrubs, ranging from forest trees to the much smaller Japanese maples, some even suitable for a rockery. Most have brilliant autumn colour or attractive young foliage and interesting bark.

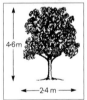

Suitable site and soil Easy to grow in most soils, but preferably a moist, cool loam. Plant in full sun or partial shade to encourage good leaf colour. Autumn hues last longer if acers are not exposed to much wind. Most Japanese maples tolerate lime.

Cultivation and care Plant from autumn to spring. No pruning required, except to remove damaged wood.

AT A GLANCE

| LOVES FULL SUN | SHADE TOLERANT | EASY TO GROW | LOVES DAMP SOIL | DECIDUOUS | LIME TOLERANT |

A. palmatum 'Atropurpureum'

A. palmatum

Propagation From seed, sown in autumn, in a cold frame.

Recommended varieties *A. griseum:* a small, slow-growing tree, to 4.6m/15ft. Peeling bark, green trifoliate leaves, brilliant red or orange autumn colour. *A. davidii:* medium-sized tree, to 9m/30ft, with white striped bark. Reddish young leaves become green later, then take on brilliant autumn colour. *A. palmatum* 'Atropurpureum': the most widely grown Japanese maple. Bronzy red leaves in summer, rich purple in autumn. *A. p.* 'Red Pygmy': very dwarf, rounded habit and thinly sectioned red leaves.

Pests and diseases Aphids may be a nuisance, especially on young growth, encouraging sooty mould fungus. Red spider mites attack young trees in hot, dry summers. Coral spot fungus may invade at points of injury, causing die back. Cut back to healthy wood and burn the diseased wood.

A DELIGHTFUL CONTAINER DISPLAY

Slow-growing, dwarf species, such as *A.p.* 'Dissectum Atropurpureum', make good container plants. Ensure efficient drainage by placing a deep layer of crocks or stones in the base of the pot, and allow space at the top for watering.

A. filipendulina 'Gold Plate'

Hardy herbaceous perennial varying in height and form from creeping rock plants to large specimens suitable for borders and cottage gardens. Most have delicate, fern-like foliage and tiny flowers in large clusters or flat heads.

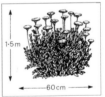

Suitable site and soil Will flourish in hot sun and tolerates most soils, provided they are not waterlogged or sour. Achilleas prefer lime but do quite well in acid conditions.

Cultivation and care Plant out between autumn and spring. Achilleas flower longer if they are dead-headed or cut for use in the house. *A. taygetea* produces a second crop of flowers if cut back severely just before flowering is over.

AT A GLANCE

LOVES
FULL SUN

GOOD FOR
CUTTING

PREFERS
LIME

A. millefolium 'Cerise Queen'

A. millefolium

Propagation Plants are best divided and replanted every two or three years, in spring, to restore their vitality. They can also be grown from seed sown in early summer.

Recommended varieties A. filipendulina: light green, feathery leaves and plate-like heads of golden flowers from mid-summer to early autumn. Good varieties include 'Cloth of Gold' and 'Gold Plate'; up to 1.5m/5ft. A. millefolium: the species can be a problem in lawns because it is so invasive, but it is very attractive. Try 'Cerise Queen' or 'Fire King'; up to 75cm/2½ft. A. tomentosa is a good rock garden species with woolly grey leaves and golden flowers from summer to autumn. Another small species, A. × wilczekii, has extremely beautiful silver-grey foliage and white flower clusters in the summer.

Pests and diseases Generally trouble-free.

DRIED FLOWER DECORATION

Pick flowers before they are fully open, tie in small, loose bunches and hang upside-down in a dry, well ventilated room.

ACONITUM/*monkshood*

A. wilsonii

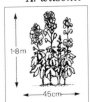

Tall, stately herbaceous perennials, most of which bear large spikes of hooded blue flowers in late summer; particularly attractive when grown among creamy yellow roses. All parts of the plant are poisonous.

Suitable site and soil   Aconitums are very easy to grow. They prefer a cool, damp location in semi-shade. They will tolerate sun—but never allow the soil to dry out.

Cultivation and care   Plant out in the spring or autumn. From the end of the second year, put a spring mulch of compost or plastic sheeting around each plant.

AT A GLANCE

SHADE TOLERANT

LOVES DAMP SOIL

POISONOUS

A. napellus 'Bicolor'

A. 'Bressingham Spire'

Propagation   By division in spring or autumn. Aconitum seed is slow to germinate and may not be true to type; for best results, sow seed as soon as it is ripe.

Recommended varieties   *A. wilsonii:* violet blue flowers from late summer to autumn; *A. 'Arendsii':* large amethyst blue flowers on strong, straight stems in late summer; 1.2m/4ft. *A. napellus:* handsome, deeply cut foliage and rich blue or purplish blooms in July/August. Particularly recommended are 'Spark's Variety', and 'Bressingham Spire'. There are pink, white or bicolor varieties available.

Pests and diseases   Generally none.

BEWARE OF POISONOUS PLANTS!

Every part of this lovely plant is poisonous, including the pollen! Always wear gloves before handling it, whether planting out, pruning or propagating.

A. kolomikta

These hardy, deciduous climbing shrubs can be grown supported on walls, old trees or pergolas. There are two very different varieties available, one which bears the fruit known as Chinese gooseberry or Kiwi fruit, and the other distinctive for its tri-coloured leaves.

Suitable site and soil   Rich and well-drained soil; not pure chalk. Best in full sun or partial shade.

Cultivation and care   Winter planting: November to March, against high wall or tree. Grown the male and female plants of *A. chinensis* next to each other to produce fruit. No need to prune, though unwanted stems can be removed in winter.

AT A GLANCE

LOVES
FULL SUN

SHADE
TOLERANT

DECIDUOUS

A. chinensis (fruits)

A. chinensis (foliage, flowers)

Recommended varieties Only two very different varieties are available. *A. kolomikta* has small, delicate leaves with very distinctive bands of colour—green, white and pink—and white, faintly fragrant flowers which tend to be hidden by foliage. *A. chinensis* (Chinese gooseberry) is vigorous, with very large dark green leaves and creamy yellow flowers, followed by hairy brown fruits which do not reach full size when grown in Britain.

Propagation Grow from seed under glass in autumn then prick out seedlings into pots in spring. Cuttings can be taken, 8-10cm/3-4in in length, of half-ripened wood.

PLANTING ACTINIDIA AGAINST A WALL

60 cm   45cm

Ensure that the base of the plant is 45cm/18in away from the wall. Dig a hole approximately 60cm/2ft deep and layer compost and bone meal in the bottom before planting. Angle plant towards wall and fill gaps around roots with compost.

A. 'Warley Rose'

This shrubby perennial rockery plant, sometimes known as 'burnt candytuft', produces short-lived clusters of tiny pink or white flowers. This evergreen plant is hardy and drought tolerant – thanks to its almost succulent leaves.

Suitable site and soil Rockery or sink garden. Full sun and any well-drained, non-acid soil.

Cultivation and care Plant in early autumn, spacing plants 15-23cm/6-9in apart, to allow for spreading. Trim lightly after flowering to prevent plants from becoming straggly.

AT A GLANCE

A. iberideum

A. grandiflorum

Propagation Divide large clumps in early spring or take cuttings in early summer. Cuttings – of soft, young shoots – need to be potted in gritty compost and placed in a cold frame.

Recommended varieties *A.* 'Warley Rose', a lovely deep pink variety, flowers April-May, for a longer period than other varieties; height and spread 15x30cm/6x12in. *A.* 'Warley Ruber' is a rounded sub-shrub with tiny blue-green leaves and racemes of deep rose-pink flowers. *A. armenum* has loose sprays of tiny pink flowers in summer. *A. grandiflorum* is the tallest, at 30cm/12in, and spreads to 45cm/18in, with very pale pink flowers in summer. *A. iberideum* has a height and spread of just 15cm/6in and small, round white flowers.

Pests and diseases None.

PLANTS FOR A GARDEN WALL

Make a special display of tiny rockery plants in the cracks of an old wall – aethionema, white rock cress (*Arabis albida*), sea pinks (*Armeria maritima*), summer starwort (*Erinus alpinus*), and *Silene maritima*.

AGAPANTHUS/*African lily*

Derek Gould

A. 'Anthea'

75 cm

60 cm

Half-hardy to hardy evergreen
herbaceous perennials with strap-like
foliage and fleshy roots. The heads of
bell-shaped flowers vary in size. Colours
range from pale blue to deep violet. The
'Headbourne Hybrids' are the hardiest.

Suitable site and soil Prefers a well drained, fertile soil and
a sunny, sheltered location, but will tolerate a degree of shade.
Plant hardy varieties in a sheltered border, use as an edging
plant, or grow in tubs in summer.

Cultivation and care Plant out in late spring, ensuring they
are firmly planted. Water generously from spring to autumn,
particularly when in flower. Divide the clumps every five or six

AT A GLANCE

LOVES
FULL SUN

SHADE
TOLERANT

GOOD FOR
CUTTING

A. *campanulatus* 'Albus'

A. *africanus*

years. Half-hardy varieties can be grown in tubs and over-wintered indoors. Give hardy varieties winter protection. Cut back stems to ground level in autumn and mulch with coarse sand.

Propagation Easiest by division in spring, just as new growth appears.

Recommended varieties *A. africanus* has pretty blue flowers in late summer; not hardy. *A. campanulatus* bears deep blue flowers in late summer; deciduous; hardy. *A.* 'Albus' is a pretty, white-flowered variety. *A.* 'Headbourne Hybrids' have pale blue to violet flowers in late summer, height 60-75cm/2-2½ft; spread 60cm/2ft.

Pests and diseases Rare.

PROTECT FROM FROST

Even hardy varieties of agapanthus need protecting during the winter, particularly in cold districts or where frosts are severe. Once they have finished flowering, cut the stems right down, level with the ground, then cover the area with coarse sand or bracken. A layer of 15cm-20cm/6-9in will protect the plant adequately from frost and cold over the winter and early spring months. Alternatively, grow in pots and take indoors.

A. reptans

Attractive, low-growing and spreading herbaceous perennials (evergreen, except in severe winters). They produce carpets of glossy oval leaves, topped by showy spikes of small, tubular flowers in late spring. Excellent ground cover.

Suitable site and soil   Use as border or edging plants, and in moist rockeries. Most luxuriant and long-lived in partial shade on a moist but well-drained soil. The variegated varieties prefer a more sunny spot.

Cultivation and care   Plant out in spring, just as new growth appears, spacing 20-30cm/8-12in apart. Water regularly to keep soil moist, but do not plant in waterlogged soil.

AT A GLANCE

SHADE TOLERANT

LOVES DAMP SOIL

EASY TO GROW

A. reptans 'Multicolor'

A. reptans 'Variegata'

Propagation Established clumps can be lifted, divided simply by pulling apart and replanted throughout the growing season, as long as the soil is moist.

Recommended varieties *A. reptans* has evergreen leaves and blue flowers in late spring. 'Atropurpurea' has a purple metallic sheen on the leaves. 'Multicolor' has bronze pink and yellow variegated leaves with glints of metallic crimson, gold, copper and cream. The leaves of 'Variegata' are grey-green and cream. *A. pyramidalis* 'Metallica Crispa', as the name suggests, has metallic-bronze coloured leaves that are crisp and curly, and blue flower spikes in late spring. Height, 10cm/4in (20cm-25cm/8-10in with flowers); spread, 45-60cm/18-24in.

Pests and diseases Usually trouble-free but ensure good drainage to prevent powdery mildew or root rot.

COLOURFUL GROUND COVER

Because of its shallow roots bugle makes attractive ground cover around small bulbs such as miniature tulips or crocuses. Choose a variety with foliage colouring which will complement the flowers that the bulbs produce.

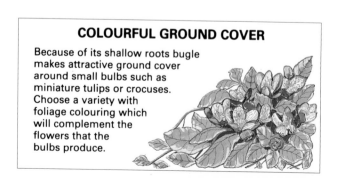

AKEBIA

A. quinata

Small family of vigorous, semi-evergreen and deciduous twining climbers; woody, with beautiful, divided leaves and brownish-purple flowers. Initially slow growing, the plants become quite rampant after two or three years.

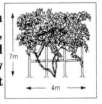

Suitable site and soil Grow over porches, walls, fences, pergolas and trellises or allow to trail through the branches of large, established trees and shrubs. Prefers a light, rich garden soil in sun or partial shade.

Cultivation and care Plant young specimens in late autumn or early spring, giving them cane supports. Young plants need winter protection. Cut back hard every few years.

AT A GLANCE

LOVES
FULL SUN

SHADE
TOLERANT

DECIDUOUS

A. *quinata*

A. *trifoliata*

Propagation A lengthy process: take 10cm/4in semi-ripe cuttings in mid summer. Once rooted, pot up singly and overwinter, preferably in a cold frame. Repot into a larger pot in spring and plant out in autumn. Seed may take up to six months to germinate. Prick out seedlings into pots, harden off, then treat as for cuttings. Or make a small cut in the under-side of one or two outer, bendy stems. Pin them down in the soil, weighting them with a large stone. Leave to root before separating.

Recommended varieties A. *quinata* has attractive, semi-evergreen leaves with five leaflets and faintly fragrant purple flowers; violet, gherkin-like fruit is produced in long, hot summers. A. *trifoliata* has smaller leaves, composed of three leaflets, and is deciduous. Flowers appear in May. Height, 4.5-6m/15-20ft; spread, 1.8-2.4m/6-8ft.

MULTIPLYING

An easy way of progagating the akebia is autumn layering of one or two outer, bendy stems. This 'plants' the stem so that roots can grow. See propagation instructions, above.

A. moly

Bulbous plants which include
onion, garlic and leeks as well as
hardy, ornamental perennials.
Most have tall stems and spherical
flower heads that are particularly
attractive to bees.

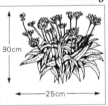

Suitable site and soil   Plant in rock gardens, borders or in
patio pots. Prefers chalk but will grow in most well-drained
garden soils. Thrives in full sun, even in very hot, dry locations.

Cultivation and care   Plant out bulbs during autumn, at a
depth twice the depth of the bulb. Mulch and feed with a
general fertilizer until well established.

AT A GLANCE

A. christophii

A. giganteum

Propagation Lift and separate bulbs in early autumn. Offsets (tiny bulblets) can be separated from the parent plant and potted up to grow on for a year or two in controlled conditions.

Recommended varieties *A. christophii* bears a spectacular display of bright, starry amethyst flowers with heads up to 25cm/10in wide in early summer. Excellent for drying. *A. moly* has tulip-like leaves and bright yellow, star-shaped flowers from early to mid summer. *A. giganteum* has strap-like leaves and deep lilac, early summer flowers in clusters 15cm/6in wide. Grows to 1.5m/5ft tall. *A. aflatunense* has rich lilac or white flowers in late spring. Grows to 90cm/3ft tall. Suitable for drying. *A. karataviense* is a good species for the rock garden at just 20cm/8in. *A. schoenoprasum* (chives) is a popular herb with a mild onion flavour.

Pests and diseases Slugs feed on the young shoots.

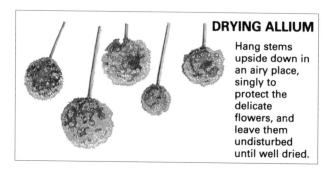

DRYING ALLIUM

Hang stems upside down in an airy place, singly to protect the delicate flowers, and leave them undisturbed until well dried.

Alonsoa warscewiczii

Half-hardy, shrubby perennials, usually grown as annuals. They have lots of small scarlet flowers and dark green oval leaves. Use in formal beds, as an edging plant or in the herbaceous border.

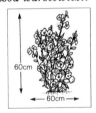

60cm

60cm

Suitable site and soil   Select a sunny location in a well-drained, fertile soil and you will be rewarded with many blooms. The more sheltered the spot, the better, as heavy rainfall and wet conditions prevent a good show of flowers.

Cultivation and care   As these plants are not fully hardy, wait until all danger of frost has passed before planting out. Be careful not to over-water them, as this hampers flowering.

AT A GLANCE

LOVES FULL SUN

GOOD FOR CUTTING

A. 'Compact Scarlet'

A. 'Compact Carpet'

Propagation Increase by sowing seeds in boxes of good compost in early spring. Keep indoors at a temperature of 16°C/60°F. Prick out and grow on until all danger of frost has passed, then plant out. Take cuttings in early autumn.

Recommended varieties *A. warscewiczii* is the best cultivated variety – a red-stemmed, compact plant with clusters of scarlet spurred flowers. *A. acutifolia* has a bushy habit and deep red flowers. *A. linearis* is a shrubby annual which has scarlet flowers through spring.

Pests and diseases Aphids should be removed immediately by spraying with warm soapy water. Fungal diseases may develop in cold, damp weather. The affected leaves should be removed immediately to prevent the spread of disease. Never put diseased leaves onto the compost heap as this will spread infection: they should be burned straight away.

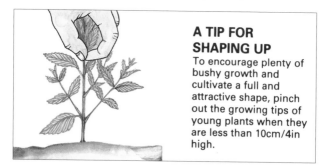

A TIP FOR SHAPING UP

To encourage plenty of bushy growth and cultivate a full and attractive shape, pinch out the growing tips of young plants when they are less than 10cm/4in high.

ALYSSUM/*gold dust*

A. saxatile 'Citrinum'

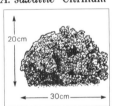

Popular rock garden perennials and real sun worshippers. They thrive in hot, open locations on poor, well-drained soil and can survive drought. Yellow flowers in late spring or early summer.

Suitable site and soil Although alyssum can grow well on relatively infertile soil, it does prefer one that is well drained. It also likes a hot, sunny location.

Cultivation and care Plant out in the spring or early autumn, spacing plants 15-30cm/6-12in apart. Cut back severely after flowering to encourage new, more dense growth. Dead-heading will extend the flowering period.

AT A GLANCE

A. *saxatile* 'Variegatum'

A. *spinosum*

Propagation   Increase by taking softwood cuttings from stems produced during current year's growth, in late spring or by sowing seed in the autumn. Divide clumps every three years to rejuvenate the plants and increase your stock.

Recommended varieties   A. *saxatile* has grey-green foliage and bright yellow flower sprays in spring or early summer. Cultivated varieties include 'Gold Dust' (chrome yellow), 'Citrinum' (pale lemon yellow) and 'Variegatum' (yellow flowers; grey-green leaves with cream margins). A. *montanum* has small, hairy grey leaves and very fragrant soft yellow flowers. A. *wulfenianum* has grey leaves and loose heads of small, bright yellow flowers. A. *spinosum* forms a spiky hummock with white or pale pink flowers that appear in early summer.

Pests and diseases   Watch out for slugs and flea beetles which will eat young plants.

SWEET ALYSSUM

The popular mauve or white-flowering bedding plant which is commonly known as sweet alyssum is not really a member of the alyssum family at all. Its botanical name is *Lobularia maritima,* but it is sometimes sold as *A. maritimum.*

A. lamarckii

Sometimes known as snowy mespilus, these very hardy deciduous trees or shrubs produce masses of small white flowers in spring. They also have striking autumn leaf colour with rich red or glossy black berries.

Suitable site and soil Select a sunny or partially shaded position. Most garden soils are suitable except those which are very dry or wet, or very chalky.

Cultivation and care Generally bought as container-grown shrubs. Prune wayward branches in winter.

Propagation Sow seed in late summer. Use pots or seed

AT A GLANCE

LOVES
FULL SUN

SHADE
TOLERANT

EASY
TO GROW

DECIDUOUS

LOVES
ALL SOIL

A. canadensis

A. laevis

trays filled with seed compost in a cold frame, if you have one. Plant out the following spring. Alternatively, layer flexible stems which grow close to the ground in autumn to early spring. Peg a stem that is still attached to the parent plant into the ground. New roots will gradually form from the layer.

Recommended varieties *A. lamarckii* is the most widely grown species, with excellent autumn colour. Both surfaces of the young leaves of *A. canadensis* are covered in dense white hairs which disappear as they mature. These two are often confused but both produce masses of white flowers in spring and red fruit in June. *A. laevis* has copper-coloured, hairless young leaves and white fragrant flowers in late spring.

Pests and diseases Fireblight can sometimes be a problem in southern areas of England.

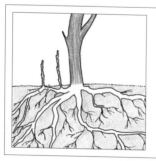

SUCKERS

Strong growing suckers may be dug up in the dormant season. These can be transplanted or potted and kept in unheated frames for a year or so until a good root system has developed.

ANACYCLUS/*Mount Atlas daisy*

A. depressus

Anacyclus is a group of very hardy perennials and annuals particularly well suited to rock gardens and sink gardens. They have a prostrate growth habit and tiny, fern-like leaves with daisy-like flowers in mid-summer.

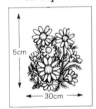

Suitable site and soil   Prefers a sunny location on a well-drained, rich soil (ideally composed of equal parts loam, sand and leaf mould). Very wet soil will harm the plant.

Cultivation and care   *A. depressus,* the alpine species, needs full sun and must not be allowed to become waterlogged. Give protection against heavy winter rains with raised panes of glass. Plant in early autumn or mid-spring.

AT A GLANCE

A. radiatus

A. depressus

Propagation Sow fresh seeds of annual species in situ in early autumn or indoors in early winter. Plant out, well spaced, in early spring. The fresh seeds of the alpine species should be sown indoors (or in a greenhouse) in seed compost with added grit and kept at a constant 10°C/50°F. Alternatively, take cuttings from non-flowering shoots in early spring or later summer. Plant out spring cuttings in early autumn; summer cuttings in the following spring.

Recommended varieties *A. depressus* is an evergreen with feathery mat-forming leaves. The white daisy-like flowers bloom throughout summer on prostrate stems. Flowers close in dull light showing red undersides of petals. *A. officinarum* and *A. radiatus* are both annuals; the former grows to 30cm/12in and the latter to 60cm/24in.

Pests and diseases Occasionally attacked by aphids.

A SINK GARDEN

Line sink with drainage material and fill with moisture retentive compost. Add a miniature rock arrangement with two or three stones. Plant up sink and mulch surface with gravel.

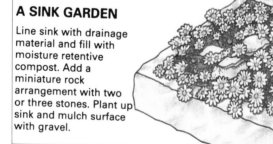

ANAGALLIS/*pimpernel*

A. tenella

Anagallis is a large family of creeping perennials and annuals that make attractive edging plants or pot plants. Tiny flowers of pink, red, blue or white are produced from summer to autumn.

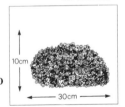

Suitable site and soil   Grow in an open, sunny location on fertile, well-drained soil. *A. tenella* requires moist conditions.

Cultivation and care   Most of the species are easy to grow but have different needs. Plant *A. tenella* in mid-spring and keep moist at all times. The perennial *A. linifolia* is not fully hardy; protect in severe cold. Plant *A. linifolia* and *A. arvensis* in late spring. If growing in pots, repot annually in early spring.

AT A GLANCE

LOVES
FULL SUN

LOVES
ALL SOIL

A. tenella 'Studland'

A. linifolia

Propagation   Increase *A. tenella* by division in spring, or by soft tip cuttings in spring or early summer. If conditions are favourable, *A. linifolia* will self-seed. Sow the fresh seeds indoors in potting compost and sand, or under glass in summer for pot plants that will flower in winter. Harden off plants intended for outside, before planting in late spring.

Recommended varieties   Hardy perennial *A. tenella* (bog pimpernel) forms a carpet of tiny, green leaves and delicate, bell-shaped, fragrant flowers in summer. Ideal for boggy ground. The low-growing variety 'Studland' has tiny, star-shaped deep pink blooms in early summer and is good for rockeries. Put bright blue *A. linifolia* in a border; height 30cm/12in. The mat-forming scarlet pimpernel, *A. arvensis*, flowers all summer.

Pests and diseases   Beware of aphids.

BORDER PLANTS

Anagallis is particularly attractive as an edging plant. At the front of a border it will get all the sun it requires as well as softening the division between the flower bed and the harder lines of the paving.

ANAPHALIS/*pearl everlasting* 43

A. yedoensis

This hardy herbaceous perennial with its silver-grey foliage and pretty heads of small, papery flowers provides ground cover for most of the year. The clusters of daisy-like flowers are pearly white and can be dried for winter decoration.

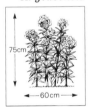

Suitable site and soil   Prefers full sun but will tolerate partial shade. Soil must be moisture-retentive. Will perform well even in poor soils.

Cultivation and care   Sow seeds where you want them to grow or set out plants in borders in spring or autumn, 30-40cm/12-16in apart. Keep watered in dry spells or it will droop and lose leaves. Cut back, if untidy, in autumn.

AT A GLANCE

LOVES FULL SUN

SHADE TOLERANT

GOOD FOR CUTTING

LOVES DAMP SOIL

EASY TO GROW

LOVES POOR SOIL

A. cinnamomea

A. yedoensis

Propagation   Increase by sowing fresh seed in autumn. Alternatively, by dividing clumps in winter or spring.

Recommended varieties   *A. margaritacea* has many heads of small, pearly-white button-like flowers and silvery-grey leaves with white margins. Flowers in mid summer. Look out for the variety sold as 'New Snow'. *A. triplinervis* is a dwarf form, ideal for the front of a border, with woolly stems, lance-shaped leaves and dense clusters of white flowers; 'Summer Snow' is a widely available variety. *A. nubigena* has woolly, silvery-grey leaves and off-white flowers, grows to a height of 20cm/8in and will tolerate dry conditions. Flowers mid to late summer. *A. yedoensis* or *A. cinnamomea* is less common, but superb for drying for everlasting flower arrangements as stems are tall and straight.

Pests and diseases   Generally trouble-free.

EVERLASTING FLOWERS

Dried anaphalis leaves have a lemony fragrance. Hang stems to dry, then strip off the leaves and crush them. Add to pot pourri or use them to fill fabric sachets to scent a linen drawer.

A. araucana

The branches of these wind-resistant conifers have upturned ends, like monkeys' tails, and grey, furrowed bark. The dark green, glossy leaves are sharply pointed and overlapping, covering the branches from tip to trunk.

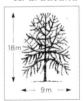

Suitable site and soil This large tree grows to 21m/70ft, with a very distinctive growth habit and is really only suitable for a large garden. You can use Araucaria as an isolated specimen in a formal or semi-formal setting. This tree is hardy and prefers a deep, moderately fertile soil that is moist but not wet. It is wind-resistant so can be planted in sites which are too exposed for many other trees.

AT A GLANCE

SHADE TOLERANT

LOVES DAMP SOIL

EVERGREEN

A. araucana

A. araucana

Cultivation and care These trees do not transplant well, so keep a young plant in a container until you have found it a permanent position. Plant out in spring or autumn. Protect from sun until well established. No pruning required.

Propagation Not really practical, as it takes three years to raise a seedling. Male and female trees must be planted in close proximity to produce fertile seeds, and this rarely happens in this country.

Recommended varieties *A. araucana* is the only species hardy enough to grow outdoors. Male trees produce clusters of catkins while females have large, spiky cones. Look out for a variety named 'Aurea', an attractive cultivar with interesting yellow variegated foliage.

Pests and diseases Generally trouble free.

BRANCHING OUT

Use any branches that fall off your tree for an attractive indoor decoration. Left in their natural state, they can form part of a stylish flower arrangement. Sprayed gold, they look lovely hung with Christmas baubles.

A. unedo

These small trees and large shrubs are moderately hardy evergreens with pretty flowers and fruits, leathery leaves and reddish-orange gnarled bark. Use as a specimen tree or as a large background plant in a border.

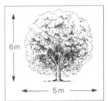

Suitable site and soil Select a sunny or partially shaded location, sheltered from drying winds. Soil should be moist but well-drained and neutral or acid, though *A. unedo* will grow equally well in a moderately alkaline soil.

Cultivation and care Plant out young trees or shrubs in spring or autumn, preferably during showery weather. Spray foliage and water frequently during dry or windy spells.

AT A GLANCE

A. andrachne

A. × andrachnoides

Support with a tree stake until well established. Choose your site well as they are difficult to transplant.

Propagation Take 15cm/6in hardwood or semi-ripe cuttings in autumn. Root in sandy soil in a cold frame and grow on in a nursery bed for a couple of seasons before planting out in spring.

Recommended varieties *A. unedo* is a small tree (6m/20ft) that provides an attractive autumn display with its whitish pink flowers and rough, spherical fruits; *A. unedo* 'Rubra' is compact, with pink flowers. *A. andrachne* has smoother fruits, grows to 4.5m/15ft and is a particularly interesting winter shrub with its peeling, reddish-brown bark, while *A. × andrachnoides* has cinnamon coloured bark all year long, often twisted branches, and flowers in spring.

Pests and diseases None.

CHOOSE CAREFULLY
The strawberry tree is a fairly expensive plant, so you will want to show it off to the full. Make it the star attraction by planting it in the centre of your lawn, but remember that it should not be moved later so you must be certain when you choose its position.

A. grandis

These daisy-like perennials, usually grown as half-hardy annuals, create a striking display of vivid colours from midsummer through to the first frosts. They enjoy a hot, dry location, making them perfect for a rockery.

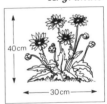

Suitable site and soil They are happy on most garden soils but will flourish on dry soil in full sun so choose a sunny location. Add sand to the soil, if necessary.

Cultivation and care Plant out seedlings in spring. Approximately one month after planting, pinch back plants by half to encourage dense growth. Flowers can be cut to make a stunning, if short-lived, display.

AT A GLANCE

LOVES FULL SUN | GOOD FOR CUTTING | EASY TO GROW | LOVES POOR SOIL | LOVES DRY SOIL

A. × hybrida

A. stoechadifolia

Propagation Sow seed indoors in early spring and plant them out in late spring. Alternatively, sow out of doors in late spring – but make sure that it is after danger of frost is past – where you want plants to grow.

Recommended varieties *A. stoechadifolia*, also known as *A.venusta*, is the blue-eyed African daisy. It is quick-growing and the white, blue-centred flowers are carried on long, thick stems. The hybrids 'grandis' have larger flowers and a sprawling habit. *A. × hybrida* is usually sold as a mixture, giving large (10cm/4in) flower heads in white, crimson, red, pink, bronze, yellow and orange, with central discs in contrasting colours. *A. breviscapa* produces flowers in an array of striking orange shades with black or purple central discs.

Pests and diseases Generally trouble free although young plants may be prone to aphid infestations.

SOIL CONDITIONS
These plants need a light soil. If your soil is heavy – a clay or loam – it can be improved by digging in some sharp sand, available from garden centres. As these plants enjoy a hot, dry location, they are ideal for planting on an exposed, sandy bank or in a rockery.

A. balearica

Sometimes known as Scotch or Irish moss, these dwarf, creeping, mat-forming annuals and perennials produce masses of white or pink flowers in spring or early summer. Some varieties are evergreen.

2.5cm

30cm

Suitable site and soil These plants prefer a sunny or partially shaded position and a well-drained, sandy soil that is not too fertile. They will fill cracks and crevices in your paths, paving and dry stone walls, and they are ideal for troughs, alpine sink gardens and rockeries.

Cultivation and care Set out young plants in spring. To revitalize old plants and increase your supply divide and

AT A GLANCE

LOVES
FULL SUN

EASY
TO GROW

LOVES
POOR
SOIL

LOVES
DRY
SOIL

DECIDUOUS

EVERGREEN

A. montana

A. purpurascens

replant perennials each spring. Remove dead flower heads to prolong the flowering period and prevent self-seeding.

Propagation Divide in spring, or sow seed in spring or autumn. Softwood cuttings can be taken in early summer and should be inserted in a light, sandy compost and potted on as soon as roots have formed.

Recommended varieties *A. balearica* prefers a shady spot and forms a dense, dark green carpet studded with tiny, star-shaped flowers in spring and early summer. Keep a check on it as it can become quite invasive. *A. caespitosa* 'Aurea' has golden foliage. *A. montana* produces masses of bold white flowers on trailing green stems. *A. purpurascens* forms a carpet of pink flowers in early summer and will tolerate light shade.

Pests and diseases None.

PLANTING IN PAVING
Arenaria balearica will spread happily between cracks in paving where the soil is likely to be sandy and well drained. These pretty little plants wil soften the hard lines of the paving and give an established look to a new path or patio.

A. maritima

This hardy evergreen perennial forms tufty clumps of grassy leaves and produces rosy pink, rounded flowers from late spring to midsummer. Varieties with long stalks are lovely in flower arrangements.

Suitable site and soil Use in the front of borders, on dry stone walls, in rock gardens or in the cracks between paving slabs. It thrives when grown in full sun on a well-drained loam or sandy soil and is particularly at home by the sea which explains the common name of *A. maritima*, the sea pink.

Cultivation and care Plant out seedlings in spring. Water moderately and do not fertilize. Cut back dead heads after

AT A GLANCE

LOVES FULL SUN

GOOD FOR CUTTING

EASY TO GROW

EVERGREEN

LOVES DRY SOIL

A. pseudarmeria

A. juniperifolia 'Bevan's Variety'

flowering to renew vigour. Divide plants in the spring to rejuvenate if centres die back.

Propagation Plants can be grown from seed sown in autumn, but seedlings are slow to develop. Plants can be divided and replanted in autumn. In summer, semi-ripe cuttings can be taken; root these in equal parts of peat and sand.

Recommended varieties *A. maritima,* the sea pink, has attractive bright pink flowers; 'Ruby Glow' and 'Bloodstone' are both a beautiful deep, rosy red, and 'Alba' is pure white. *A. juniperifolia* has pinkish-lilac flowers; 'Bevan's Variety' is a pretty deep pink variety. *A. pseudarmeria* flowers from early to late summer. 'Splendens' is a long-stemmed hybrid, good for cutting.

Pests and diseases Generally trouble free.

ARMERIA WITH ALPINES

Armeria looks particularly attractive in a natural setting with other alpines. Grow it in an alpine bed and surround it with gravel to improve drainage. You can grow armeria in an alpine trough, rockery or sink garden, too.

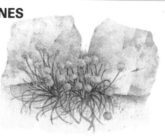

A. dioicus (syn. A. sylvester)

These hardy perennials produce clumps of broad, fern-like foliage and magnificent creamy white flower heads in summer. They make excellent feature plants and look spectacular around the edge of a pond.

Suitable site and soil   As this is a tall, stately plant, it is best planted as an isolated specimen in the back of a border or in a woodland setting. It also looks very effective near water. It is vigorous and will grow well in most conditions, but prefers a deep, moist soil in sun or partial shade.

Cultivation and care   Plant out seedlings in spring. Mulch well and ensure plants receive plenty of water throughout the

AT A GLANCE

LOVES FULL SUN

SHADE TOLERANT

GOOD FOR CUTTING

EASY TO GROW

LOVES DAMP SOIL

LOVES ALL SOIL

A. dioicus (syn. A. sylvester)

A. dioicus 'Kneiffii'

growing season, in early summer. Cut the stems right back to ground level in October.

Propagation Sow seed in autumn or early spring. (Female plants produce the best seed-heads.) Plants can be divided in spring or autumn.

Recommended varieties A. dioicus (also known as A. sylvester and A. vulgaris) has long, fern-like foliage and forms a clump up to 1.8m/6ft high and 1.2m/4ft wide. The male form of the plant, with the most elegant flowers, is more widely available than the female. 'Kneiffi' is a dwarf variety, 90cm/3ft high, with finely cut leaves and wiry shoots. (Garden centres may label aruncus by is old name, Spiraea aruncus.)

Pests and diseases Generally free from disease, aruncus may suffer from sawfly larvae which eat holes in the leaves.

EFFECTIVE PLANTING

Use aruncus as an accent plant in a large flower bed or near water. Damp or moist soils offer ideal growing conditions.

Though short-lived, the flowers, with their fern-like foliage, are extremely attractive and showy.

A. japonica

4.5 m — 1.2 m

These graceful, hardy evergreens with hollow, jointed stems and rustling, lance-shaped leaves are fast growing. Once established, the clumps form excellent focal points or barriers to use as screens against unsightly areas.

Suitable site and soil Bamboos need a sunny position but preferably one protected from cold winds. Plant in moist, fertile soil in a sheltered spot.

Cultivation and care Plant in late spring in moist soil and take care not to allow the roots to dry out. For small gardens, invasive varieties can be grown as specimens in tubs or other containers to confine their spread.

AT A GLANCE

EVERGREEN

LOVES DAMP SOIL

LOVES FULL SUN

LOVES ALL SOIL

A. nitida

A. viridistriata

Propagation   Divide plants in late spring or early autumn and replant in moist soil.

Recommended varieties   *A. japonica* (Japanese bamboo) is a vigorous species which is good for screening and one of the hardiest bamboos, but it can be too invasive in a small garden. Height 2-4.5m/7-15ft. *A. murielae* makes a fine specimen as a focal point in a lawn. It has slender arching canes and dark green leaves. Height 2-3m/7-10ft. *A. nitida* is similar but has dark purple canes. *A. variegata* is a smaller bamboo (height 1m/3ft) with handsome dark green and white striped leaves. *A. viridistriata* has brightly striped green and gold leaves. Height 1.2m/4ft. *A. anceps* is another invasive variety with tall arching stems which branch out at the nodes. Excellent for screening. Height 3-4.5m/10-15ft.

Pests and diseases   Generally trouble free.

A NATURAL SCREEN

A line of bamboos makes an elegant natural screen, dividing one area of the garden from another. Such a screen is useful for hiding an unsightly compost heap, dustbins or a vegetable garden from view.

A. major

These hardy herbaceous perennials are
ideal for flower arranging because of
their striking shapes and distinctive
colours. They last well when cut
and also look dramatic growing in
mixed borders.

Suitable site and soil   Astrantias will tolerate most soil types
but do need moisture. They thrive in shade, but will tolerate
sun as long as the soil remains moist.

Cultivation and care   Plant astrantias between mid-autumn
and early spring. Support the stems with twiggy sticks if your
plants are in an exposed position and cut them back after
flowering in late summer.

AT A GLANCE

A. maxima

A. carniolica 'Rubra'

Propagation Increase the number of your plants by dividing and replanting the roots of well-established plants in spring or autumn. Alternatively you can sow seed, although this method of propagation is quite lengthy. Sow seeds into trays at the end of summer, and overwinter them in a cold frame. Prick out the seedlings the following spring and then in the summer plant them out in a nursery bed. They will be ready for your borders the following spring.

Recommended varieties *A. major* has attractive foliage and starry flowers, greenish-white at the centre, surrounded by a green collar; they grow to 60cm/2ft tall. *A. maxima* has lovely pale pink flowers and bright green leaves. *A. carniolica* has tiny star-like white flowers which are ideal for cutting. 'Rubra' is a variety with a plum-red collar.

Pests and diseases Generally trouble-free.

GROW EXTRA FOR CUTTING

Astrantia's star-like, slightly ethereal quality makes it particularly attractive in flower arrangements, so grow more than you think you will need and plant the spares in an out-of-the-way spot, for cutting.

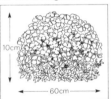

A. 'Bressingham Pink'

These popular hardy perennials are best known for their ability to cling to dry stone walls and clothe them with bright colour in spring. They are excellent, too, on banks and rock gardens and they thrive in limy soil.

Suitable site and soil   Plant in an open position with good drainage and lime. Aubrietas will root in crevices in walls.

Cultivation and care   Plant between autumn and spring. Trim back after flowering to encourage a tidy, compact habit.

Propagation   Divide old plants and replant them in position directly. Take 5cm/2in basal cuttings in autumn, winter in

AT A GLANCE

A. 'Red Carpet'

Aubrieta in three colours.

peat and sand in a cold frame (if you have one) and plant out in spring. Aubrietas seed themselves but the resulting seedlings will usually grow into less colourful and attractive plants than the parent.

Recommended varieties   Aubrietas form small mounds and are often trailing. They are all spring flowering and of the same size: height 15cm/6in and spread 45-60cm/18-24in. 'Bressingham Pink' and 'Mary Poppins' are double pinks. 'Bressingham Red' has large rose-red flowers. 'Red Carpet' is a deep red. Violet blues include 'Dr Mules' and 'Carnival'. Pale lavenders include the lovely 'Cascade Lilac'. 'Gurgedyke' is a bright, deep purple.

Pests and diseases   White blister can cause white powdery blisters on leaves and stems. Downy mildew causes yellow blotches on the leaves.

WALL PLANTING

Aubrietas are excellent wall plants and will cascade down, providing eye-catching curtains of lovely spring colour. Firm the roots in place in crevices with limy soil and water well until established.

A. japonica 'Gold Dust'

A family of hardy evergreen shrubs,
grown for their attractive gold and
green foliage and red or yellow berries.
Not only are they resistant to severe
frost, they are also at home in shade
and tolerant of pollution.

Suitable site and soil You can grow aucubas in any soil
providing it is not waterlogged. They can be grown in full sun
to deep shade. They also make good container plants. Aucubas
are particularly useful plants for town gardens and seaside
areas.

Cultivation and care Aucubas are very easy to grow. Plant
in autumn or spring, making sure you have plants of both sexes

AT A GLANCE

EASY
TO GROW

SHADE
TOLERANT

LOVES ALL
SOIL

A. japonica

A. japonica 'Maculata'

if you want berries (for the best show, plant three females to one male). No pruning necessary.

Propagation Propagate by semi-ripe cuttings in late summer. Insert 10-15cm/4-6in long cuttings, with a heel, in a peat and sand mixture. In spring place them in a nursery bed to mature when they are ready to plant in their permanent positions.

Recommended varieties *A. japonica* (spotted laurel) has narrow, leathery leaves, and in many varieties these are variegated. 'Crotonifolia', male, is boldly speckled with yellow; 'Gold Dust', female, is spotted with gold. The males carry insignificant spring flowers and the females usually have red berries, though 'Fructu-albo' has yellow-white ones.

Pests and diseases Generally trouble free.

PLANTING UNDER TREES

Aucubas are ideal for planting in the shady area under a deciduous tree. In winter, their bright cream or gold with green variegated leaves and red berries create a focus, diverting attention from bare branches.

BERBERIS/*barberry*

B. darwinii

Easy-to-grow shrubs. The evergreens have small glossy leaves and clusters of orange or yellow flowers which appear in spring, followed by blue-black berries. Deciduous species have red berries and brilliant autumn colour.

Suitable site and soil Tolerates poor, shallow soils. Deciduous species prefer full sun for good autumn colour. Evergreens thrive in sun or partial shade.

Cultivation and care Plant between autumn and spring. Trim evergreen hedges after flowering, deciduous hedges before growth in early spring or autumn.

AT A GLANCE

B. thunbergii

B. darwinii

Propagation   Propagate by cuttings, preferably with a heel between midsummer and autumn. Root in peat/sand mix and grow on in pots for a couple of years before planting.

Recommended varieties   *B. darwinii* is the most widely grown evergreen. It forms a bushy shrub 3m/10ft high with prickly leaves and masses of orange/yellow flowers in clusters in spring, followed by blue-black berries. *B.* × *stenophylla* 'Coccinea' is a dwarf form with unusual red buds and coral-pink flowers in spring. It has round purple berries in autumn. *B. thunbergii* is a deciduous bush with pale yellow flowers, small red berries and bright red autumn colour. 'Atropurpurea Nana' has reddish-purple leaves and a dwarf habit to 45cm/ 18in. 'Aurea' is another dwarf with golden-yellow young leaves.

Pests and diseases   Generally trouble-free.

HEDGING AND BIRDS
B. darwinii and other varieties with spines or prickly leaves make good impenetrable hedges and are easy to grow even in poor, shallow soils. The dark green, holly-like leaves make good wind protection and, after planting 30-37.5cm/12-15in high plants 45-60cm/18-24in apart, prune the top quarter to make the plants bush out. The blue autumn berries which make this such an attractive hedge are also very appealing to common garden birds – they make excellent winter food for them – so berberis is a good 'green' plant to encourage wildlife to your garden.

BERGENIA/*elephant's ears*

B. cordifolia

Formerly known as *Saxifraga* or *Megasea*, these hardy, evergreen border plants have glossy, large leathery leaves which develop purplish tinges in autumn and winter. They make useful groundcover plants and tolerate drought.

Suitable site and soil   Easy to grow in sun or semi-shade. It tolerates almost all soil conditions, including lime but leaf colour actually improves on poor soil in full sun.

Cultivation and care   Plant between autumn and spring and leave undisturbed until the clumps grow overcrowded. Remove flower stalks and old leaves as they die to prolong the flowering season and generally improve appearance.

AT A GLANCE

LOVES FULL SUN | SHADE TOLERANT | EASY TO GROW | EVERGREEN | LOVES ALL SOIL

B. crassifolia

B. cordifolia

Propagation   Stocks of bergenia can be easily increased by division. Separate the roots of crowded clumps into individual plants and replant in autumn or spring.

Recommended varieties   *B. cordifolia* has prominent rounded leaves like waterlily leaves with heavy hanging heads of lovely bell-shaped reddish-purple flowers in spring on rich red stalks. *B. purpurascens* has purplish-red or pink flowers held above the leaves. 'Ballawley', a more vigorous hybrid, has larger fuchsia-red flowers. *B. crassifolia* has fleshy leaves and branching panicles of large pink flowers.

Pests and diseases   Generally none, though occasionally leaf spot fungus produces brown blotches on the leaves in damp conditions.

CREATING A WINTER GARDEN

Many of the bergenia family flower in very early spring or even late winter. This is a time when the garden can look at its bleakest but there are, in fact, many plants which are at their best now. You can use bergenia to underplant deciduous shrubs and trees – one very attractive partnership would be to plant under the winter-flowering cherry, *Prunus subhirtella autumnalis*, which has either white or pale pink flowers. Many shrubs are also in flower now – camellias, witch-hazel, viburnum, magnolia and rhododendrons – as well as many heathers and bulbs.

BUDDLEIA

B. davidii

These hardy deciduous or evergreen shrubs or small trees are grown for their masses of scented summer flowers. Easy to grow on most soils, most species have flowers of various shades of purple, red or occasionally white.

Suitable site and soil All species prefer full sun. They are lime tolerant, but will thrive best in a well-drained, loamy soil, though some varieties actually prefer chalky or limestone soils.

Cultivation and care Plant buddleia in the autumn or spring. *B. davidii* and varieties which flower on the current year's growth should be pruned hard before growth starts in spring. *B. globosa* should be pruned after flowering.

AT A GLANCE

LOVES ALL SOIL

EASY TO GROW

LOVES FULL SUN

LIME TOLERANT

NEEDS PRUNING

FRAGRANT

B. d. 'White Profusion'

B. alternifolia

Propagation   Take semi-hardwood cuttings with a heel in late summer. Root in an equal mixture of peat and sand in boxes in a cold frame. Pot on into John Innes No. 1 or similar compost the next spring and plant out the spring after that.

Recommended varieties   *B. davidii* (butterfly bush) and its many named varieties flower in mid to late summer and scent the air with their heady perfume which is popular with butterflies. 'Royal Red' is a rich, glowing rose-red form, 'Black Knight' an even deeper red, and 'White Cloud' has dense clusters of pure white flowers. *B. alternifolia* is a deciduous small tree or shrub up to 6m/20ft in height which is seen to best advantage in early summer. *B. globosa* is the orange-flowered species, a vigorous evergreen especially useful in seaside gardens.

Pests and diseases   Generally trouble-free.

THE BUTTERFLY BUSH

Make a buddleia tree the central feature of a wildlife garden.

Butterflies, especially the Tortoiseshell and Red Admiral, will flock to it. Butterflies will feed on windfalls from fruit trees so plant one or two nearby. A mini-meadow will encourage Gatekeepers and Meadow Browns to roost, feed and breed.

BUXUS/*box*

B. sempervirens

3m

1.5 m

These slow-growing, dense evergreen shrubs or small trees are usually cultivated as hedging, or as edging for formal gardens. Along with yew, they are used for mazes and for topiary.

Suitable site and soil   Box will grow in most soils, including chalk, and is happy in full sun or light shade.

Cultivation and care   Choose plants approximately 30cm/12in high and plant in autumn or spring 30cm/12in apart for hedging. Cut back lightly in summer using sharp shears to encourage branching. Box is good for topiary and trees should be clipped into shape in late summer.

AT A GLANCE

EVERGREEN

NEEDS PRUNING

LOVES ALL SOIL

EASY TO GROW

B. sempervirens

B. s. 'Suffruticosa'

Propagation Cuttings taken as soon as the young growth becomes firm in late summer or early autumn will root quite easily in an equal mixture of peat and sand in boxes indoors or outside in a cold frame.

Recommended varieties *B. sempervirens* (common box) has small, glossy, dark green leaves growing in pairs up the stems and scented pale yellowy-green flowers hidden amongst the foliage in spring. *B. s.* 'Argentea' has even smaller leaves with white edges. *B. s.* 'Latifolia Maculata' has slightly larger leaves with yellow variegation. *B.* 'Suffruticosa' is the smallest of all and best for really low edging.

Pests and diseases A variety of leaf spot fungi can cause pale brown spotting on the leaves and rust can cause darker brown discolouration. Leaf suckers can cause distortion of young leaves.

A TRADITIONAL HERB GARDEN

Turn a herb garden into a knot garden by surrounding it with a low box hedge. Choose some favourite herbs: thyme, rosemary, sage, feverfew, lavender and savory are all suitable.

CALTHA/*marsh marigold/kingcup*

C. palustris

These hardy herbaceous perennials have bright yellow or white flowers in the early spring. They grow best at the margins of ponds or in boggy ground. They are often the first plants to bloom in the water garden.

Suitable site and soil Calthas prefer an open, sunny aspect and a slightly acid soil which must be kept moist and cool at all times if the plants are not actually in water.

Cultivation and care Plant out between spring and autumn in wet soil or in containers 15cm/6in deep in water. If the leaves begin to look messy as the summer wears on, these may be removed.

AT A GLANCE

LOVES
FULL SUN

LOVES
DAMP
SOIL

EASY
TO GROW

C. palustris 'Plena'

C. palustris alba

Propagation After plants have finished flowering, in late spring or early summer, divide and replant the roots. The crowns should separate quite naturally.

Recommended varieties *C. palustris* (height 60cm/24in) has cup-shaped, golden-yellow flowers, early in the spring, and grows in water up to 15cm/6in deep. *C. p.* 'Plena' is a smaller but showier variety with double flowers and does best as a marginal plant. *C. p. alba* is a white variety which blooms in early spring and again in late summer. *C. polypetala* (height 60cm/24in) will sprawl given time and so is best for a fairly large pond. It has heart-shaped leaves and deep golden flowers. *C. leptosepala* is a less common variety with rounded, light green leaves and starry late spring flowers.

Pests and diseases Rust fungus may develop on leaf surfaces and stalks.

MARGINAL PLANTING

Calthas, like other marginal plants, like to be in shallow water. When you plan your pond make a shelf for their pots which will be covered by only 7.5cm/3in of water.

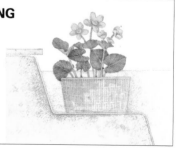

CEANOTHUS/*Californian lilac*

Ceanothus 'Cascade'

These evergreen (spring flowering) and deciduous (summer flowering) trees and shrubs are grown for their clusters of beautiful blue panicles of tiny flowers. Some are only suitable for warmer areas.

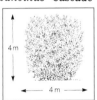

4 m

4 m

Suitable site and soil   Ceanothus prefer a sheltered site and well-drained soil. Most are lime tolerant but will not flourish in poor, shallow chalky soil.

Cultivation and care   Plant out in spring or autumn. Cut back deciduous species in spring to within 8cm/3in of old wood. Cut dead wood from evergreens in spring.

AT A GLANCE

LOVES FULL SUN

NEEDS PRUNING

DECIDUOUS

EVERGREEN

C. 'Autumnal Blue'

C. Burkwoodii

Propagation Increase from cuttings in midsummer. Overwinter in a cold frame, pot on in the spring and plunge the pots in the ground for planting out the following autumn.

Recommended varieties *C.* 'Cascade', an evergreen, has arching branches and long panicles of pale blue flowers in late spring and early summer (height and spread 4m/12ft). It needs a warm, sheltered position. *C.* × 'Gloire de Versailles' (height and spread 2m/6ft) is a deciduous shrub with long panicles of scented, pale blue flowers. C. 'Burkwoodii' is a dense evergreen shrub (height 1.8m/6ft, spread 2m/6ft) which is frost hardy. It has dark, glossy leaves and bright blue flowers from midsummer to mid-autumn.

Pests and diseases The stems may be infested with scale insects. Alkaline soil conditions may cause chlorosis. Frost damage causes die-back, so grow in a sheltered position.

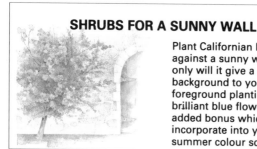

SHRUBS FOR A SUNNY WALL

Plant Californian lilac against a sunny wall. Not only will it give a glossy background to your foreground planting, its brilliant blue flowers are an added bonus which you can incorporate into your summer colour scheme.

CHOISYA/*Mexican orange blossom*

C. ternata

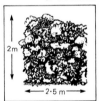

Two or three varieties of this small family of evergreen shrubs are commonly grown. They owe their popularity to their shiny, bright green leaves and pretty white, sweet-scented flowers, produced in late spring.

Suitable site and soil   Choisyas are easy to grow in any well-drained garden soil. They prefer full sun but they can also be grown in partial shade.

Cultivation and care   Plant in spring in a position sheltered from wind. A sunny wall is ideal for this purpose. After flowering, prune lightly to thin out straggly shoots. Prune any frost-damaged shoots in spring.

AT A GLANCE

LOVES FULL SUN

NEEDS PRUNING

FRAGRANT

EASY TO GROW

EVERGREEN

C. ternata

C. ternata 'Sundance'

Propagation   Take half-ripe cuttings in late summer and pot in equal parts of peat and sand. Over-winter in a cold frame, if you have one, and plunge the pots in their flowering positions the following spring.

Recommended varieties   *C. ternata* (height 1.5-1.8m/5-6ft, spread 1.8-2.4m/6-8ft) has very attractive, glossy green leaves. The leaves and the clusters of white flowers are both very fragrant. The main flush of flowers appears in spring but can frequently continue throughout the year to autumn. 'Sundance' has bright yellow leaves.

Pests and diseases   Choisyas are generally free of pests. The most likely damage is from frost, so protect from cold and wind if possible. The plants may also be attacked by honey fungus, a soil-borne disease. Remove dead and dying plants, including roots, and change the soil before any new planting.

PLANTING ON A PROTECTED PATIO

With a plant like the Mexican orange blossom which comes from the warmest of climates, bear in mind that it is liable to suffer damage in cold winters. It is a good idea to grow it in a pot which can be moved to a sheltered spot for the winter. The ideal place is a sunny patio where it should have the necessary protection from the wind and frost. You could even celebrate its Mexican origins by planting it in a paint decorated terracotta pot!

CORNUS/*dogwood*

C. alba 'Sibirica'

A reliably hardy and easy to grow
family of shrubs and small trees
grown primarily for their coloured
bark, which is particularly decorative
in winter, or less commonly for their
attractive foliage, fruit and flowers.

Suitable site and soil   Any fertile garden soil. Many species
like a moist soil. A few flowering species will not tolerate
chalky soils. They like a position in full or partial sun.

Cultivation and care   Prune long stemmed varieties that are
grown for the colour of their stems right back to within a few
centimetres of the base in spring. Flowering varieties do not
require pruning.

AT A GLANCE

LOVES FULL SUN   GOOD FOR CUTTING   EASY TO GROW   LOVES DAMP SOIL   DECIDUOUS   LOVES ALL SOIL

C. alba 'Variegata'

C. alba 'Aurea'

Propagation   As the seeds may take up to 18 months to germinate it is easier to take cuttings in summer and plant them in pots containing a mixture of equal parts peat and sand. You can plant them directly into the soil.

Recommended varieties   All *C. alba* varieties have long red stems which bring colour to the garden in winter. Choose 'Variegata' which has white and green variegated leaves in summer or 'Aurea' for its golden yellow leaves. *C. stolonifera* 'Flaviramea' has long yellow stems. *C. mas* (Cornelian cherry) is the most common flowering variety. It produces yellow flowers on bare branches in early spring. The attractive fruits are edible. *C. kousa* 'Chinensis' is an elegant flowering shrub which does not like chalky soil. *C. florida* 'Rubra' has rosy pink flowers and the young leaves have a reddish tinge.

Pests and diseases   Generally trouble free.

ALL-YEAR COLOUR

The rich red stems of a *Cornus alba* 'Sibirica' show in winter if the shrub is pruned firmly every March or April. If fully grown, cut the young shoots down to the main stem. If coppiced, trim almost to ground level.

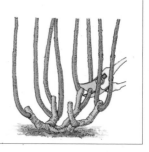

CORTADERIA/*pampas grass*

C. selloana 'Sunningdale Silver'

A family of evergreen perennial grasses with stately, silvery plumes and sharp-edged, arching leaves. Pampas grass is easy to grow and makes a splendid specimen plant for a lawn.

Suitable site and soil Cortaderia will grow in any deep, well-drained fertile soil. It prefers a sunny site and protection from cold winds.

Cultivation and care Plant in borders or as a specimen plant in lawns in the spring. Trim down with shears in early spring but wear gloves to remove dead leaves as the edges of the

AT A GLANCE

C. selloana 'Pumila'

C. selloana 'Gold Band'

leaves are very sharp and can cause painful cuts.

Propagation Divide and replant in spring.

Recommended varieties *C. selloana* forms a dense thicket of leaves 1.8-2.7m/6-9ft high. Individual leaves can be up to 1.5m/5ft long. Individual leaves can be up to 1.5m/5ft long. In autumn tall, silky flower plumes tower over the leaves. 'Sunningdale Silver' is an attractive variety with long-lasting, creamy plumes in late summer. 'Pumila' is easily obtained and great for a small garden, growing to a compact 1.2m/4ft. 'Gold Band' (also sold as 'Aureo-lineata') has gold-striped leaves; 'Rendatleri' silver-purple plumes. *C. richardii*, available at specialist nurseries, is more compact (height 1.5-2.7m/5-9ft) with green leaf rib and flowers.

Pests and diseases Generally trouble-free.

SPECIMEN PAMPAS GRASS

Pampas grass looks best when treated as a specimen plant. If you do grow it in a mixed border, try to surround it with darker shrubs which form a good backdrop for the pampas grass's silvery flowers.

CORYLUS/*hazel*

C. avellana 'Aurea'

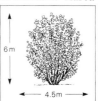

6 m

4.5 m

A family of hardy deciduous trees and shrubs, best known for their edible nuts which appear in the autumn. Some also have decorative catkin flowers which add interest to the garden in the late winter.

Suitable site and soil Hazels prefer full sun or semi-shade, a certain amount of shelter from cold winds and a rich but well-drained soil.

Cultivation and care Container-grown plants can be planted at any time. Cut out suckers as they arise. Prune young plants back by half in early spring.

AT A GLANCE

LOVES FULL SUN

NEEDS PRUNING

DECIDUOUS

C. avellana 'Contorta'

C. maxima 'Purpurea'

Propagation Propagate by layers in the autumn and do not sever until well rooted – this can take a year.

Recommended varieties *C. avellana* (height 6m/20ft) has yellow male catkins on bare branches in midwinter. 'Aurea' has soft yellow leaves and 'Contorta', the corkscrew hazel, has interesting twisted branches covered, in late winter, with pendant pale yellow catkins. *C. maxima* is a shrub (height 3m/10ft) with heart-shaped leaves and large nuts (filberts). The form 'Purpurea' has intense purple leaves and catkins. *C. tibetica*, the Tibetan hazel, is difficult to find but has distinctive spiny husks enclosing the nuts and is wide spreading, sometimes producing a thicket of stems.

Pests and diseases Weevils may eat the immature nuts and leaves. This can in turn lead to brown rot fungus. Mildew can also cause defoliation.

GATHERING NUTS

Wait until the husks which enclose the nuts begin to turn brown before you pick them. Spread them out on newspaper in a dry, airy place to store until you are ready to eat them. They will keep for several months.

COTINUS/*smoke bush*

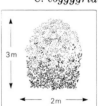

C. coggygria

Medium-sized shrubs with rounded
leaves and beautiful autumn foliage
ranging in colour from orange to red.
The name 'smoke bush' comes from
the feathery flower heads, which turn
smoky grey later in the year.

Suitable site and soil   The smoke bush grows well in a sunny
position in ordinary garden soil. If the soil is too rich, the autumn
leaf colour will not be so pronounced, so do not add manure to
the soil, although leaf mould or peat can be used as a conditioner
at planting time. Shade also inhibits colour change.

Cultivation and care Plant container-grown plants at any
time, but preferably in early autumn or mid-spring. Pruning is

AT A GLANCE

LOVES
FULL SUN

EASY
TO GROW

DECIDUOUS

C. coggygria 'Foliis Purpureis'

C. coggygria 'Notcutt's Variety'

unnecessary apart from the removal of dead wood or over-long new growths.

Propagation Take semi-ripe cuttings 10-13cm/4-5in long in late summer. Insert in 50/50 peat and sand by volume and place in a cold frame. Pot up the following spring. Alternatively layer long shoots in late spring or early summer.

Recommended varieties *Cotinus coggygria* is green-leaved with brilliant autumn tints. Best varieties are 'Purpureus' with purple-pink flower heads and 'Notcutt's Variety' with purple leaves. The hybrid, 'Grace', (available at specialist nurseries) has light purple leaves and is very vigorous.

Pests and diseases Powdery mildew can occur on purple-leaved forms. Spray fortnightly with a systemic fungicide in hot, dry weather to prevent spores surviving.

BACKGROUND FOLIAGE

Grow your smoke bush against a dark green foliage background to show off both the purple foliage and the red autumn colour and smoky haze of the late flower heads of a green-leaved form.

CRATAEGUS/*hawthorn*

C. monogyna

Tough, thorny, long-lived, large shrubs or small trees with small, lobed leaves and clusters of scented flowers in white, pink or red. It produces small, crimson fruits in autumn and is deciduous.

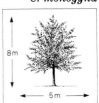

Suitable site and soil   Any garden soil, preferably in sun, is suitable. *C. monogyna*, the common thorn, is ideal for hedges. All plants stand up to wind, including salt-laden gales by the sea, and tolerate drought well.

Cultivation and care   Plant common hawthorn in winter, 35cm/14in apart for hedges. Container-grown hawthorns for ornamental use can be planted at any time, but autumn and

AT A GLANCE

LOVES
FULL SUN

LOVES ALL
SOIL

DECIDUOUS

EASY
TO GROW

C. prunifolia

C. oxyacantha 'Paul's Scarlet'

spring are best. Pruning is not often necessary but cut old plants back very hard in winter if desired

Propagation　Species (not named varieties) can be propagated by sowing seeds as soon as they are ripe. They should be placed outside in shade and kept weed-free. Patchy germination is likely to take two years. Cuttings do not strike (root), so named forms must be increased by grafting.

Recommended varieties　Forms of *C. momogyna* are difficult to find. *C. prunifolia* has white flowers followed by large 'haws' (some specimens have brilliant autumn colouring). *C. laevigata* (syn. *C. oxyacantha*) varieties include 'Paul's Scarlet' with scarlet flowers and 'Plena' with double white flowers.

Pests and diseases　Sometimes suffers from fireblight for which there is no cure. Caterpillar damage is usually not severe.

HAWTHORN FOR HEDGES

Hawthorn for hedges is commonly grown from seed. Place the seed tray against a north-facing wall with wire netting as protection until germinated. Although slow and patchy in the first couple of years, growth is quick thereafter.

Deutzia

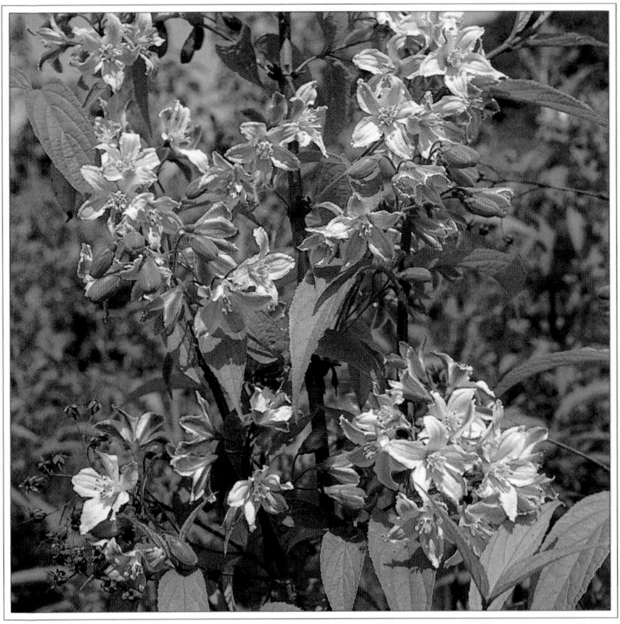

D. × *hybrida* 'Magicien'

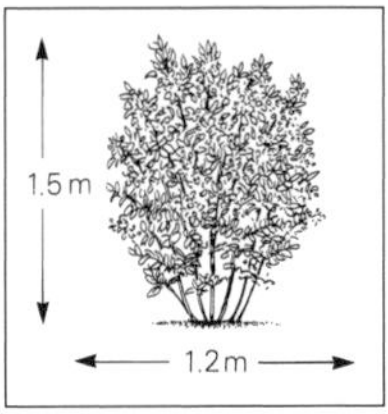

Popular, easy-to-grow, deciduous shrubs with pretty cup, bell or star-shaped flowers in white or shades of pink in early summer. They need protection from frost which can damage young growth.

Suitable site and soil Deutzias will grow in any well-drained soil and will tolerate very chalky conditions. They thrive in sun or light shade but prefer some protection from frost.

Cultivation and care Plant in late autumn or winter. Pruning is important and in the first year the shrub should be thinned out to its strongest stems. Afterwards, cut back to new growth after flowering each year.

AT A GLANCE

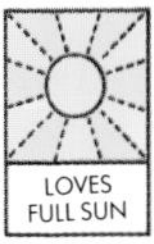

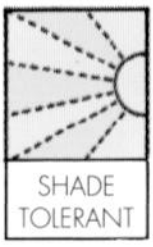

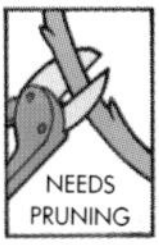

D. × rosea 'Carminea'

D. × elegantissima 'Rosealind'

Propagation Take 7.5-10cm/3-4in cuttings in summer, over-winter in a cold frame; or take 25-30cm/10-12in hardwood cuttings in autumn and plant outdoors. Hardwood and semi-ripe cuttings root straight into the ground.

Recommended varieties *D × hybrida* is a group of graceful, erect shrubs (height 1.8m/6ft) including 'Magicien' with starry pink flowers edged in white. *D. × rosea* is smaller (90cm/3ft) and the form 'Carminea' has petals pale pink inside, dark on the outside. *D. pulchra* (height 2.4m/8ft) has long panicles of blush-pink, lily-of-the-valley type flowers and peeling orange-brown bark. *D. × elegantissima* has fragrant pink flowers. The variety 'Fasciculata' is deep pink and 'Rosealind' is carmine. *D. scabra* is also a popular garden species, with 'Pride of Rochester' a notable variety (height 1.5m/5ft).

Pests and diseases Generally trouble-free.

A DEUTZIA HEDGE

For an attractive and unusual hedge, plant a line of 10-15cm/4-6in cuttings in autumn where you want the hedge to grow. Remove the lower leaves before planting and space the cuttings 15-30cm/6-12in apart.

ERANTHIS/*winter aconite*

E. hyemalis

A hardy, tuberous-rooted perennial, one of the earliest and brightest spring flowers, with golden-yellow, buttercup-like flowers, framed by bright green leaves. In mild areas, winter aconites flower in midwinter.

Suitable site and soil Any reasonably well-drained soil is suitable for winter aconites but they should never be allowed to dry out altogether, so a heavy loam is best. They do well in sun or partial shade beneath deciduous trees and shrubs.

Cultivation and care Plant 2.5cm/1in deep in groups in late summer or early autumn. Keep well watered during the spring growing period.

AT A GLANCE

LOVES FULL SUN   SHADE TOLERANT   LOVES DAMP SOIL

E. × tubergenii 'Guinea Gold'

E. cilicica

Propagation Once established, winter aconites spread and naturalize freely. Lift tubers as leaves die down, break into separate sections and replant immediately.

Recommended varieties *E. hyemalis* is the most common species and especially good for naturalizing. It has yellow flowers, surrounded by a ruffled collar of green leaves, on short stems (height 10cm/4in) from midwinter. *E. × tubergenii* is more robust with more golden, slightly larger flowers (up to 2.5cm/1in across) and flowers a little later in early spring. A recommended form is 'Guinea Gold' which has large, deep yellow, fragrant flowers that appear in early and mid spring. *E. cilicica* has bronze-tinted foliage and pink stems.

Pests and diseases Birds sometimes damage the flowers as they open. Too much disturbance after planting and lack of moisture in spring can halt growth.

NATURALIZED WINTER FLOWERS

A carpet of winter aconites and snowdrops is a real pleasure in the coldest months of the year. Plant groups of both together under shrubs or trees and give them space to spread.

ERYNGIUM/*sea holly*

E. maritimum

A family of perennials suitable for borders where their unusual metallic-looking, thistle-like flowers and spiny foliage can make a feature. They like dry, sandy soil and are good for seaside gardens.

45cm

45cm

Suitable site and soil Eryngiums like full sun and sandy, even poor, soil. They are wind resistant.

Cultivation and care Plant between autumn and spring. Some varieties need twiggy sticks for support. Cut down to ground level after flowering, but remember some varieties are also interesting in the autumn, when the flower heads are brown and dry.

AT A GLANCE

LOVES FULL SUN

GOOD FOR CUTTING

EASY TO GROW

LOVES POOR SOIL

LOVES DRY SOIL

E. variifolium

E. alpinum

Propagation By root cuttings in midwinter. Overwinter in a cold frame in an equal mix of sand and peat for planting out in the following autumn. Alternatively, sow seeds in spring for planting out in autumn.

Recommended varieties *E. maritimum* is the wild sea holly with silver-green leaves and metallic blue flowers from mid-summer to autumn (height 45cm/18in). *E. × oliverianum* has steely blue stems and deep blue flowers surrounded by prickly bracts (height 60cm/2ft). *E. variifolium* is an evergreen with glossy green, white-veined leaves, metallic blue flowers and white bracts. *E. tripartitum* is less spiny than other varieties with blue-grey flowers (height 75cm/2½ft). *E. alpinum* (height 75cm/2½ft) has heart-shaped basal leaves and deeply cut stem leaves.

Pests and diseases None.

NATURAL SUPPORTS

Many of the taller plants, including some varieties of sea holly, need support as they grow. You can, of course, use canes but twig sticks form much cheaper and less obtrusive supports for the plants.

EUCALYPTUS/*gum*

E. gunnii

Fast-growing trees and shrubs with attractive, mottled bark, prolific scented flowers and strongly aromatic foliage. Many grow into large trees, but they can be pruned hard regularly to make ornamental shrubs.

Suitable site and soil   Plant in full sun, with protection from cold winds, in good ordinary or acid soil which remains moist but not waterlogged. If growing as a specimen tree, underplant with shade-loving plants, or for a more compact specimen grow in a large container.

Cultivation and care   Plant very young specimens in summer and dig in bonemeal or other fertilizer. Do not allow to dry out.

AT A GLANCE

LOVES FULL SUN   NEEDS PRUNING   GOOD FOR CUTTING   FRAGRANT   EVERGREEN

E. niphophila

E. niphophila

Stake to prevent wind rock and check ties regularly. Cut back annually in spring to required size or to encourage young foliage.

Propagation   They can be grown from seed, but this can be unreliable so buy pot-grown plants.

Recommended varieties   *E. gunnii* (cider gum) is the most common form with round, silver-blue young leaves, changing to sage green in mature plants. It can grow to a large tree up to 21m/70ft but responds well to pruning to a small tree or shrub. White flowers appear in midsummer. *E. niphophila* (alpine snow gum) is a smaller (up to 6m/20ft) evergreen with flaking bark which makes a beautiful mottled effect. It has thick, glossy green leaves, sometimes tinted bronze when young and clusters of white flowers in early summer.

Pests and diseases   Young trees: attack by blue-gum suckers.

JUVENILE FOLIAGE

The young leaves of eucalyptus are often more attractive than the mature ones. To keep these pretty, rounded, blue leaves, cut back all annual growth in spring. Use the prunings for flower arrangements.

FATSIA/*Japanese aralia*

F. japonica

A single species genus, fatsia is a theatrical, evergreen shrub with huge, fingered, glossy leaves. When fully grown it demands a conspicuous location to show it to best advantage.

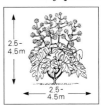

2.5 - 4.5m

2.5 - 4.5m

Suitable site and soil Large fatsias are spectacular so choose a site where it can stand out. Most fertile well-drained soils will suit the plant and it needs sun or partial shade. In cold areas, grow in a sheltered spot.

Cultivation and care Fatsia does not require pruning. Plant out in early autumn or spring. If container-grown re-pot in spring.

AT A GLANCE

SHADE TOLERANT

EVERGREEN

PREFERS WELL-DRAINED SOIL

F. japonica

F. japonica 'Variegata'

Propagation Can be grown from seeds in autumn or spring but cuttings of sucker shoots taken in early to mid spring are much easier.

Recommended varieties *F. japonica* itself has dark-green, hand-shaped leaves often more than 30cm/1ft across, and there is just one variant *F.j.* 'Variegata' with cream-coloured edges to the leaves. The plant also produces large, round clusters of creamy white flowers in sprays in autumn followed by small black fruits. It is often grown in pots in cool conservatories, where it thrives, but it also does well outdoors if the soil is good and the plant is given a sheltered position, in sun or shade. It grows well in cities.

Pests and diseases Generally trouble-free but in very cold conditions can suffer frost damage, which may distort the leaves, making small holes in them.

TOWN SHRUB

In a sheltered town garden where space is limited, fatsia looks terrific grown close to an interestingly textured wall. The enormous leaves provide bold contrast against brick or painted surfaces.

GEUM/*avens*

G. chiloense 'Mrs Bradshaw'

Handsome hardy perennials with long-lasting, bowl-shaped flowers in bright and often unusual colours, appearing from early to midsummer and sometimes later. Their divided foliage is fresh green.

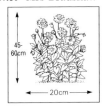

Suitable site and soil   Plant in any garden soil, preferably in groups of three or more, 35cm/14in apart at the front of a sunny border. The alpine *G. montanum* should have a gritty soil in the rock garden. *G. rivale* thrives in moist soil.

Cultivation and care   Plant between autumn and spring in sun or part shade. Little care is needed beyond removal of dead flower stems.

AT A GLANCE

LOVES
FULL SUN

GOOD FOR
CUTTING

EASY
TO GROW

G. rivale 'Leonard's Variety'

G. × *borisii*

Propagation Sow seed in late winter and place in a cold frame. Prick out into pots and plant in autumn (the following spring for *G. montanum*). Named varieties should be divided in early spring. All geums are the healthier for division every three years, and young plants often flower until autumn.

Recommended varieties Look for varieties of *G. chiloense* such as 'Prince of Orange'; 'Mrs Bradshaw', with scarlet, semi-double flowers (height 80cm/32in); and 'Lady Stratheden' with yellow, double flowers (height 45cm/1½ft). *G. rivale* has nodding flowers. Good varieties include 'Coppertone', with single, orange-tinted copper flowers; 'Leonard's Variety' with pink flowers. The hybrid *borisii* has pure orange, single flowers, 2.5cm/1in wide. 'Georgenburg' is a paler form.

Pests and diseases Trouble-free.

COLOUR CONTRAST

Show off the orange colours of *G.* × *borisii*, whose bowl-shaped flowers appear in early summer, with the grey foliage of *Senecio cineraria*, also known as *Cineraria maritima*.

GYPSOPHILA/*baby's breath*

G. paniculata 'Bristol Fairy'

Hardy perennials, and annuals, with airy clouds of dainty, small flowers, ideal for arrangements and bouquets and for following spring flowering plants; some make bright alpines for the rock garden in summer.

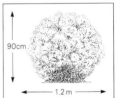

Suitable site and soil Grow border gypsophilas in full sun. They are good perennials in warmer areas and in deep, well-drained soils (but are less so in damp and cold). Plant behind patches of spring bulbs and perennials that become bare in summer. Plant alpines in sun in a gritty, well drained soil.

Cultivation and care Gypsophilas are easily grown, given the right site and soil. Leave them undisturbed to build up into

AT A GLANCE

LOVES FULL SUN

GOOD FOR CUTTING

EASY TO GROW

LIME TOLERANT

LOVES DRY SOIL

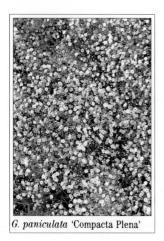

G. paniculata 'Compacta Plena'

G. repens 'Dorothy Teacher'

large specimens. Border plants should be 90cm/3ft high and 1.2m/4ft wide when mature. Take care with young plants, as varieties of *G. paniculata* may have been root grafted.

Propagation Sow seed of border gypsophilas in late spring in an outdoor seed bed. Take soft basal cuttings of named varieties in spring and root in a heated propagator. Take soft cuttings of alpines in spring and root in a cold frame.

Recommended varieties Good border gypsophilas are *G. paniculata*, with tiny, white flowers; 'Bristol Fairy'; and the longer-lived 'Compacta Plena'. 'Rosy Veil' is a first-class border/alpine hybrid. Alpine types include forms of the long- flowering, pink or white *G. repens* e.g. 'Dorothy Teacher'. *G. elegans* is a hardy annual and 'Covent Garden' a selected strain.

Pests and diseases Trouble free.

TAKE-OVER BID

Gypsophilas are good for following spring-flowering plants such as oriental poppies which flower in late spring. When the poppies fade and are cut down, gypsophila flower stems can take over.

HEBE/*veronica*

H. pinguifolia 'Pagei'

These semi-hardy evergreen shrubs are enjoyed for their attractive flowers and decorative foliage. Ranging from low to tall, willowy bushes they can be used as specimens in tubs or as hedges.

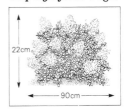

Suitable site and soil   Plant in an open, sunny position in any well-drained garden soil which does not dry out. Tender species need protection from frost and wind.

Cultivation and care   Plant between autumn and spring. Deadhead after flowering and trim back any leggy shoots that spoil compact hedge shapes in spring.

AT A GLANCE

H. 'Autumn Glory'

H. albicans 'Red Edge'

Propagation Take 8cm/3in cuttings from non-flowering stems in summer: overwinter in peat and sand in a cold frame. Pot up rooted cuttings in spring ready for planting out hardy species in autumn. In winter protect tender species.

Recommended varieties *H. pinguifolia* 'Pagei' is hardy and compact, with small, silvery-grey leaves and white flower spikes. *H.* 'Autumn Glory' has a height and spread of 60-90cm/2-3ft. It has violet-blue flower spikes from summer to autumn. *H. albicans* 'Red Edge' is a dwarf plant with grey leaves tinged with red and white flowers. *H.* 'Margaret' has blue flowers in summer that fade to white.

Pests and diseases Usually pest free but, in winter, usually in greehouse conditions, leaf damage is caused by leaf spot and downy mildew. Plants may succumb to honey fungus.

MAKING A HEBE HEDGE

You can use well-rooted cuttings of many hebes to make an informal hedge. Plant about 10cm/4in apart. Pinch out the central shoot to encourage side shoots. At end of summer cut back flowering stems.

HELIANTHEMUM
rock rose, sun rose

H. nummularium 'Firedragon'

Helianthemums are a family of fast-growing evergreen dwarf shrubs and herbaceous plants best suited to a sunny rock garden. They are very free flowering and throughout the summer produce colourful blooms.

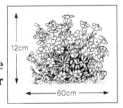

Suitable site and soil   Helianthemums prefer full sun and will grow in any ordinary dry, poor or sandy soil. They do well in rock gardens, between paving stones and even in walls.

Cultivation and care   Plant between autumn and spring. As they spread so vigorously, they should be pruned back after flowering to preserve a neat appearance and prevent them from swamping other plants.

AT A GLANCE

H.n. 'Wisley Pink'

H.n. 'Wisley Primrose'

Propagation Take heel cuttings in summer. When rooted, pot up in loam-based compost and overwinter in a cold frame in pots of equal quantities of peat and sand. Pinch out the tips so the plants will bush out. Plant them out in the spring.

Recommended varieties *H. nummularium* is the common helianthemum and has a number of excellent garden varieties which are all low growing (height 10-15cm/4-6in) and spread up to 60cm/24in. 'Afflick' has green foliage and orange-yellow flowers. 'Firedragon' has flame-coloured flowers. 'Praecox' has grey foliage and yellow flowers. 'Wisley Pink' has soft pink flowers and grey foliage. 'Wisley Primrose' has grey-green foliage and primrose yellow flowers. 'Mrs C. W. Earle' has dark green foliage and scarlet flowers with yellow bases.

Pests and diseases In particularly hot weather, powdery mildew may coat the leaves.

SHEARING HELIANTHEMUMS

Use shears to cut back sun roses hard after flowering, removing at least a third of the plant. This will control its invasive habit and will often produce a further flowering in the early autumn.

HELIOPSIS/*orange sunflower*

Heliopsis scabra

This family of annuals and herbaceous perennials has yellow daisy-like flowers – hence its common name of orange sunflower. It is a good border plant with its brilliant yellow summer flowers.

Suitable site and soil   Plant in any ordinary garden soil in a sunny position in the middle or towards the back of a mixed bed or border.

Cultivation and care   Plant between autumn and spring. Cut down the flowering stems in late autumn after all flowering has finished. The taller varieties may need some staking – tie in gently, leaving room for growth.

AT A GLANCE

H. scabra 'Golden Plume'

H. scabra 'Light of Loddon'

Propagation Divide and immediately replant the roots between autumn and spring.

Recommended varieties *H. scabra* is a hardy perennial with single, yellow, daisy-like flowers 7.5cm/3in across carried at the ends of their long stems. It has long, coarsely toothed leaves and rough stems and leaves (height 90-120cm/3-4ft). Its varieties include: 'Golden Plume' with double golden-yellow flowers (height 105cm/42in); 'Light of Loddon' has single bright yellow flowers and is very free flowering; 'Orange King' has bright orange flowers; 'Summer Sun' is 1m/3ft tall with golden-yellow double flowers; 'Gigantea' is 1.2-1.5m/4-5ft tall with semi-double golden-yellow flowers.

Pests and diseases Generally trouble free.

BLUE AND YELLOW SUMMER BORDER

Heliopsis is a good border plant and its bright yellow flowers mix particularly well with the cooling shades of blue. Plant with cornflowers and the blue drifts of love-in-a-mist.

IBERIS/*candytuft*

I. sempervirens

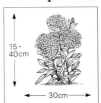

15 – 40cm

30cm

Easy to grow and tolerant of difficult conditions, these popular perennials and hardy annuals make a bright splash of colour on rockeries, in the flower border and as edging for paths.

Suitable site and soil   Candytuft thrives in full sun in well-drained soil, but it does tolerate poor soil conditions.

Cultivation and care   Plant perennial candytuft in autumn or spring. Deadhead perennials and annuals to encourage flowers.

Propagation   Sow annual seeds in flowering position in

AT A GLANCE

LOVES FULL SUN

SHADE TOLERANT

FRAGRANT

EASY TO GROW

LOVES POOR SOIL

LOVES DRY SOIL

I. 'Fairy Mixed'   *I. sempervirens* 'Snowflake'

autumn or spring and thin out. Also sow under glass or indoors in seed trays in autumn for planting out in late spring. Take 5cm/2in soft wood cuttings from non-flowering stems of perennials in midsummer. Plant in peat and sand in a cold frame. Pot up rooted cuttings to overwinter; plant out in spring.

Recommended varieties   Annual candytuft provides summer scent as well as dense floral ground cover. They vary in height from 15cm/6in to 40cm/15in and should be thinned to 23cm/9in. 'Flash Mixed' has a range of deep colours. 'Fairy Mixed' are shorter and in pastels. 'Giant Hyacinth Flowered White' comes in densely packed white flower spikes. Perennial *Iberis sempervirens* 'Snowflake' has pure white blooms in spring and makes a bright display on walls and rockeries.

Pests and diseases   Holes in leaves caused by flea beatle. Generally unaffected by pests and disease.

COOL WHITE

Use white varieties of candytuft to cool the hot colours of a yellow-orange border of gazania, gaillardia and *Cosmos* 'Bright Lights'. Or for an elegant white border mix with white foxgloves.

JUNIPERUS/*juniper*

Juniperus communis

Many of the members of this large family of slow-growing evergreen trees and shrubs are suitable for smaller gardens. They range from upright trees to creeping ground cover. There is a wide variety of leaf colour.

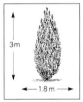

Suitable site and soil   Plant in full sun and in any ordinary, well-drained garden soil. Most junipers thrive on chalk and dry soil.

Cultivation and care Plant in the spring. No pruning or staking is required.

Propagation Take heel cuttings in autumn and overwinter in

AT A GLANCE

J. communis 'Depressa Aurea'

J. communis 'Compressa'

a peat/sand mixture under glass. Alternatively, pick the berries in autumn and plant the seeds in pots.

Recommended varieties *J. communis* has prickly, silver-backed leaves. *J.c.* 'Depressa Aurea' is a good ground cover with yellow leaves. *J.c.* 'Compressa' is a dwarf shrub (30-60cm/1-2ft) which grows slowly into a column and is excellent for the rock garden. *J. chinenis* is a column-shaped tree and varieties suitable for the smaller garden include 'Aurea' (up to 7.5m/25ft) with golden-yellow leaves and 'Kaizuka' whose spreading branches give it an unusual architectural quality. *J. virginiana* is a slender conical tree of up to 6m/20ft; 'Glauca' is silvery-grey. *J. scopulorum* 'Skyrocket' is a narrow tree with blue-grey foliage. *J. horizontalis* has long branches which form a carpet of dense ground cover.

Pests and diseases Scale insects may damage the foliage.

A CONIFER FOR A SMALL GARDEN

Though many conifers grow into majestic trees, junipers such as *J. scopulorum* 'Skyrocket' offer the conifer's distinctive shape and colour in even a small garden.

KERRIA

Kerria japonica

This very hardy deciduous shrub is well known for being particularly easy to grow virtually anywhere. Its cheerful, bright butter-yellow flowers appear plentifully in the spring on slim, arching stems.

Suitable site and soil Kerrias thrive in ordinary garden soil and in sun or partial shade. They are good shrubs to grow against walls or fences and, in very cold areas, they need the protection of a sunny wall.

Cultivation and care Plant during mild weather between autumn and spring. The flowers appear on stems thrown up from ground level the previous year so, after flowering, cut some of

AT A GLANCE

Kj. 'Pleniflora'

Kj. 'Variegata'

the old stems back, right down to ground level (see box below).

Propagation Take cuttings in the autumn or separate rooted suckers from the parent plant. Overwinter in a cold frame in an equal parts peat/sand mix.

Recommended varieties *K. japonica* has bright green, graceful stems and rich yellow, buttercup-like flowers. It is very free flowering (height and spread 1.2-1.8m/4-6ft). *Kj.* 'Pleniflora' is known as 'bachelor's buttons' and has double orange-yellow flowers over a slightly longer period than the species and it is more vigorous, reaching up to 2.4m/8ft. *K. j.* 'Variegata' is a small shrub (90cm/3ft) with a spreading habit, single yellow flowers and creamy-white variegated leaves.

Pests and diseases Generally trouble free.

PRUNING FOR NEXT YEAR'S FLOWERS

Create new growth for next year's blooms by pruning hard after flowering. Cut some old flowering stems right down to ground level and thin out newer stems.

KOLKWITZIA

Kolkwitzia amabilis

A genus of only one species, *K. amabilis,* the beauty bush, is a graceful, twiggy bush with elegant, peeling brown stems and delightful foxglove-like flowers. It has a fragile look but is very hardy.

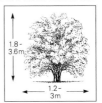

Suitable site and soil Plant in full sun and any well-drained garden soil. Kolkwitzia thrives on chalk, for which it is one of the best deciduous shrubs.

Cultivation and care Plant in mild weather in late autumn or early spring. Prune every year after flowering by removing older, straggly stems at ground level, leaving good new growth to encourage flowering.

AT A GLANCE

K. 'Pink Cloud'

K. 'Rosea'

Propagation Softwood cuttings can be taken in early summer. Alternatively, take heel cuttings in late summer. Both should be overwintered in a cold frame in an equal mix of peat and sand. Plant outside the following spring and move to their final flowering positions the following autumn, once well established.

Recommended varieties *K. amabilis* (height 1.8-3.6m/6-12ft; spread 1.2-3m/4-10ft) forms a dense clump of drooping branches, covered with large quantities of soft pink flowers with yellow throats. The flowers appear in late spring or early summer. 'Pink Cloud' and 'Rosea' are both clones with superb, bell-shaped, pink flowers. The dark green leaves of this shrub are oval, hairy and toothed.

Pests and diseases Shoots of young plants may die back in very cold weather.

ATTRACTIVE WINTER BARK
The beauty bush is principally grown for its display of delicate pink flowers. But its attractive peeling brown stems can also make a handsome background for the taller spring bulbs.

LABURNUM/*golden rain*

A. × watereri 'Vossii'

Hardy deciduous trees that flower in spring with cascading trails of pea-like, yellow flowers. They offer light shade for other plants and are useful as seasonal screening, but all parts of the plant are poisonous.

Suitable site and soil Thrives in sun or shade in well-drained garden soil. Stake young trees and water them in droughts.

Cultivation and care Plant bare-root plants between autumn and spring, container-grown plants at any time. After spring flowers are over, remove any dead or damaged branches.

Propagation In autumn sow seed into trays of seed compost

AT A GLANCE

LOVES FULL SUN

DECIDUOUS

POISONOUS

LOVES ALL SOIL

L. anagyroides

L. × watereri 'Vossii'

and place in a cold frame or cool greenhouse. Once seedlings are established prick them off into boxes and later into a well-drained site. Next autumn plant them into their final growing positions. Plants from seed are often inferior; it is really best to buy new plants. Hybrids do not come true from seed.

Recommended varieties For a free-flowering tree with very long racemes of flowers in early summer choose *L × watereri* 'Vossii', a hybrid of garden origin. *L. anagyroides* (common laburnum) flowers in spring. 'Aureum' has yellow leaves that turn to green in autumn and there is also a weeping or pendulous form, 'Pendulum', that is pretty in a small garden. *L. alpinum* (Scotch laburnum) has an upright form.

Pests and diseases Leaf-cutter bees cut circles in leaves. Susceptible to honey fungus: flowers fail to open; browning and die-back follow.

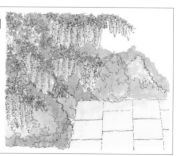

SEASONAL SCREEN
Laburnums can grow to 10m/30ft but their spreading shape and pendulous flowers provide a light, dappled screening effect in spring and summer. Use them for privacy in a front garden or by a patio.

LAURUS/*bay laurel or sweet bay*

Laurus nobilis 'Aurea'

A hardy evergreen shrub, bay laurel is popular as a formal container-grown, half-standard used to ornament front doorways. It can, however, grow to more than 6m/20ft. Its leaves are much used in cooking.

6 m

4 m

Suitable site and soil Grow in a sheltered position in sun or partial shade with good drainage and average soil. For container growing, use a 45cm/18in tub with good drainage and a loam-based compost. Top dress annually.

Cultivation and care Plant in spring; repot container plants also in spring. Clip shaped plants two or three times during summer. Remove dead or damaged leaves.

AT A GLANCE

LOVES FULL SUN

EVERGREEN

LOVES ALL SOIL

PREFERS WELL-DRAINED SOIL

L. nobilis

L. n. 'Aurea'

Propagation In late summer take semi-ripe heel cuttings. Root them in pots of peat and sand and overwinter in a cold frame. In spring, pot on until they reach a suitable size to plant in a container or in the ground.

Recommended varieties *L. nobilis* has both male and female forms. Both have tiny yellowish flowers in spring, but female trees produce dark black berries in autumn. *L. n.* 'Aurea' (golden bay) with butter-gold leaves and *L. n. angustifolia* (willow leaf bay) with narrow twisted leaves, are available from specialist nurseries.

Pests and diseases Scale insects on undersurface of leaves, especially in container plants, produce sticky and sooty substance. Leaf scorch in winter is caused by cold if not in a sheltered situation. Can be fatal for young plants. Leaf curl and woolly aphid can also be a problem.

MAKING A STANDARD
Grow main shoot to height of finished shape. Pinch it out when it is 15cm/6in higher. Keep laterals to 2-3 leaves. At right height allow laterals 5-6 leaves. Keep pinching out until bushy shape develops.

LYTHRUM/*purple loosestrife*

L. salicaria 'Robert'

A fully hardy group of herbaecous perennials and some annuals, they are most commonly represented in the garden by varieties of two of the herbaceous perennials. They have small, star-shaped flowers.

Suitable site and soil While these plants do well in almost any soil and in full sun, they are best in partial shade and in a moist and fairly heavy soil. They do well in a border where they can show off but make excellent waterside plants or bog garden plants.

Cultivation and care Plant out in mid autumn or in late winter to early spring. Cut them back in autumn.

AT A GLANCE

L. virgatum 'Rose Queen'

L. virgatum 'The Rocket'

Propagation Increase varieties by division in spring and species by seed in spring or division in spring or autumn.

Recommended varieties Varieties of *L. salicaria* (purple loosestrife) have an average height of 1.2m/4ft and a width of 60cm/2ft. Good varieties which flower through summer include two clump-forming perennials, *L. s.* 'Firecandle' ('Feuerkerze') which has rose-red flowers thickly borne in spikes and is 1m/3ft high by 45cm/18in wide and *L.s.* 'Robert', growing to 75cm/2½ft high by 45cm/1½ft wide with bright pink flowers. *L.s.* 'Lady Sackville' bears rose-pink flowers in summer. Successful varieties of the summer-flowering *L. virgatum* include *L.v.* 'Rose Queen' with light magenta flowers, *L.v.* 'Rosy Gem' and *L.v.* 'The Rocket', 1m/3ft by 45cm/1½ft wide with attractive magenta flowers over mid-green, narrow leaves.

Pests and diseases Usually no problems.

BOG GARDEN
If you have patch of damp ground by a stream or a pool, plant one of the lythrum varieties, such as *L.s.* 'Firecandle' or *L.v.* 'The Rocket'. They give bright colour to an otherwise dull area.

MAHONIA

Mahonia aquifolium

A very useful and attractive group of evergreen, mostly fully hardy shrubs with yellow flowers, some species of which are fragrant. The foliage gives good cover and the flowers bring welcome colour in winter and spring.

Suitable site and soil Most well-drained yet moist good soils will do, preferably in a site where there is partial shade. Most mahonias can tolerate full sun but some, including *M. japonica*, get scorched leaves in full sun.

Cultivation and care Plant out in early autumn or spring.

Propagation By seed, cuttings, layers or division.

AT A GLANCE

M. aquifolium

M. japonica

Recommended varieties *M. aquifolium* (Oregon grape), 1.2m/4ft high by 1.5m/5ft wide, has cheerful fragrant yellow flowers in spring and in autumn it has grape-like berries. The leaves are dark green and turn purplish in winter. *M. japonica* is one of the best winter-flowering large shrubs and can grow to about 2.4m/8ft producing sprays of delicate, bright yellow, strongly fragrant flowers in winter. Its statuesque shape gives it year round appeal and like *M. aquifolium* it can do well in less than favourable conditions. An excellent and widely available variety is *M.* 'Charity', which is tall and upright with dense foliage of large green leaves. It grows up to 3.5m/11½ft and has long spikes of fragrant, deep yellow winter flowers. Site it in a sheltered position.

Pests and diseases Usually no problems other than fungal infections such as powdery mildew and leaf spot. Rust can also affect mahonias.

COVER IN THE SHADE

Plant *M. aquifolium* in a bed against the north wall of a house. It is slow growing and will provide good cover and flowers. Generally well behaved, it can sometimes be invasive.

MALUS/*flowering crab apple*

Malus 'Golden Hornet'

This group of hardy deciduous trees bears attractive spring flowers and ornamental apples in autumn. Grown as standard trees they fit well into most small gardens. Crab apples are used to make delicious jams and jelly.

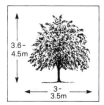

3.6-4.5m

3-3.5m

Suitable site and soil Plant in full sun in an open sunny site in average soil with good drainage. Enrich the soil with bulky organic matter.

Cultivation and care Stake young plants until they are growing well. Mulch in spring and keep base grass-free. In late winter prune out dead and damaged wood so that the tree has a well-balanced branch system.

AT A GLANCE

LOVES FULL SUN

DECIDUOUS

PREFERS WELL-DRAINED SOIL

M. 'John Downie'

M. 'Lemoinei'

Propagation New stocks are created by grafting onto certain rootstocks. Best to buy new plants.

Recommended varieties Malus vary in flower colour, leaf colour and fruit colour. M. 'Golden Hornet' has white flowers and a profusion of golden fruit in autumn. M. 'John Downie' is a narrow, upright shaped tree with fiery orange-red and yellow fruits. For best reddish pink flowers, coppery-red leaves and pinky-red fruits grow M. × purpurea, M. 'Lemoinei' or M. 'Profusion'. M. floribunda has pale pink flowers.

Pests and diseases Malus is affected by the same pests and diseases as edible apples. Aphids attack young shoots in spring. Capsid bugs distort buds, leaves and fruit. Moth caterpillars and red spider mites damage leaves, and fruits are damaged by codling moth and apple sawfly. In spring, apple mildew causes damage to leaves.

FRUIT AND JELLY
Most edible apples need another apple tree planted nearby for cross-pollination. In limited space, grow a malus as a pollination partner and use its ornamental fruits to make crab apple jelly.

NEPETA/*catmint*

Nepeta × faassenii

These hardy perennials produce attractive spikes of soft blue flowers over a long period in summer. Nepeta is useful as an edging plant. It looks pretty tumbling over low walls and spilling onto paving and patio.

Suitable site and soil   Plant in a sunny open position in well-drained ordinary garden soil.

Cultivation and care   Cut back the old growths in autumn and every few years lift and divide clumps, in spring.

Propagation   Grow from seed sown in autumn or by division. Stem tip cuttings can be taken in spring.

AT A GLANCE

LOVES FULL SUN

EASY TO GROW

LOVES DRY SOIL

Nepeta 'Six Hills Giant'

N. hederacea 'Variegata'

Recommended varieties *Nepeta × faassenii* (sometimes listed as *N. mussinii*) grows to form a bushy mound of greyish leaves with 15cm/6in long spikes of soft blue flowers from early summer through to late summer. It grows to a height of 45cm/18in and its aromatic leaves are attractive to cats, hence its common name. 'Six Hills Giant' is taller, growing up to 90cm/3ft. Its flowers are a deep violet blue. 'Superba' grows to 1m/3ft. Both tall varieties suit the back of a deep border and may need careful staking. *N. grandiflora* with its neat and erect form is useful in a mixed summer border and has many small lavender blue flowers. *N. hederacea* (ground ivy), also sold as *Glechoma hederacea*, is useful only as a dense evergreen ground cover under trees, but can be invasive; the variegated form *N.h.* 'Variegata' makes a pretty trailing display in window boxes and hanging baskets.

Pests and diseases Trouble free except for powdery mildew.

CAT-NAPPING
Attract cats away from plant beds with a block of nepeta in a sunny position. The cats will roll among its leaves, rub their faces in the flowers and foliage, and generally show their pleasure.

NYMPHAEA/*water lily*

Nymphaea 'Firecrest'

A group of hardy and tropical deciduous perennial water plants of which a few hardy species and many hardy varieties and hybrids are cultivated in outdoor ponds for their lovely flowers and green leaves.

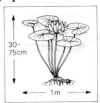

Suitable site and soil   Easy to grow in a rich, fibrous loamy soil in a sunny position in still water. If the soil is poor, use a slow-release water lily fertilizer. Depending on variety, plant directly in a clear pond between 10cm/4in and 1m/3ft deep.

Cultivation and care   Plant in spring. Remove dead leaves in autumn to prevent them fouling the water as they decompose. Keep water clear where young plants are growing.

AT A GLANCE

Nymphaea alba

N. 'Marliacea Chromatella'

Propagation   Increase old plants by division in late spring. Take care when dividing tuberous rooted plants.

Recommended varieties   There should be a large choice at a good specialist nursery; choose the colour you want for the depth of pool you have. A good variety for a pool up to about 60cm/2ft deep is *N.* 'Firecrest', with deep green leaves and pink flowers up to 13cm/5in across. A good variety for a shallow pool up to about 30cm/1ft is *N. pygmaea* 'Alba' with dark green leaves and small white flowers up 3cm/1in across. For deeper pools of about 90cm/3ft, try *N. alba,* with white flowers, or *N.* 'Marliacea Chromatella' with dark green leaves flecked with maroon and bronze, whose large yellow flowers are up to 20cm/8in across.

Pests and diseases   Prone to aphids, water lily beetles, leaf spot and stem rot.

PLANT IN A BASKET

Plant young water lily plants in a plastic basket supported on bricks or flat stones, as they do best when the water above them is not too deep. The basket can be gradually lowered as the plant grows.

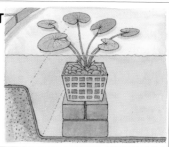

OENOTHERA/*evening primrose*

Oenothera missouriensis

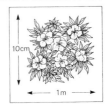

This group of perennials and biennials and annuals includes hardy plants grown for their short-lived, delicately scented flowers. They do well in borders, and some are excellent rock-garden plants.

Suitable site and soil   Most soils in a sunny position will do, as long as they are well drained.

Cultivation and care   Plant out between autumn and spring. Mark sites covered with certain varieties of the plant as they die completely away in winter and might be mistakenly dug up. Perennial species should be cut down to ground level in late autumn. Water liberally when weather is hot and dry.

AT A GLANCE

LOVES FULL SUN

FRAGRANT

EASY TO GROW

PREFERS WELL-DRAINED SOIL

O. tetragona

O. biennis

Propagation Grown from seeds or can be divided in spring. It can also be grown from cuttings taken in spring.

Recommended varieties *O. missouriensis* is a popular hardy perennial evening primrose with large flowers for its size; it does well in a border or in a rock garden. It grows to about 10cm/4in high and the spread is 45cm/18in or more. The wide, bell-shaped yellow flowers open in the evening throughout the summer and are up to 8cm/3in wide. The summer-flowering *O. tetragona* is a bushy branching plant that does well in dry summers and grows to 60cm/2ft with many yellow flowers about 3cm/1in across. *O. biennis* (1m/3ft), the true evening primrose, has masses of light yellow flowers, short-lived but produced all summer, set off by red sepals.

Pests and diseases Young plants may suffer from eelworms; otherwise plants might suffer from mildew.

YELLOW AND PURPLE

O. missouriensis looks especially good in a border when planted in front of purple-leaved sage, *Salvia officinalis* 'Purpurascens'. Plant at least five *O. missouriensis* in a border to make a good show.

OLEARIA/daisy bush

Olearia × haastii

These hardy and less than fully hardy flowering evergreen shrubs, natives of New Zealand, are grown for their daisy-like flowers in summer and year-round attractive leaves. Some are grown as hedges, especially by the sea.

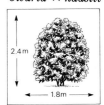

2.4 m

1.8m

Suitable site and soil   Most well-drained soils and a bright sunny spot will suit the daisy bush. Some shelter is often necessary but where the sea keeps the air warmer, more exposed sites are fine.

Cultivation and care   Plant out in autumn. Pruning is not really necessary except for those used as hedges, which should be trimmed in spring.

AT A GLANCE

LOVES FULL SUN

EVERGREEN

PREFERS WELL-DRAINED SOIL

O. × scilloniensis

O. semidentata

Propagation Increase from semi-ripe cuttings in late summer.

Recommended varieties *O. × haastii* is an excellent hardy town shrub not bothered too much by soil quality or even pollution. It grows to 2.1m/7ft high by 2.7m/9ft wide with small oval leaves and abundant, small white daisy-like flowers produced in midsummer. *O. × scilloniensis* grows to 1.2m/4ft and produces large white flowers from late spring to midsummer. *O. semidentata* is a compact rounded evergreen 3m/10ft across with heads of lilac flowers in summer.

Pests and diseases Usually no problems.

SEASIDE HEDGE

Plant *O. macrodonta* to provide good cover and shelter in a mild seaside position where it will grow into a large and sturdy hedge. Trim every spring to keep its shape. Its silver-white flowers appear in summer.

PHILADELPHUS/*mock orange*

Philadelphus 'Beauclerk'

The large, white, heavily-scented flowers of this group of mostly fully hardy deciduous shrubs resemble orange blossom in scent and flower colour and put on a bold display in early and midsummer.

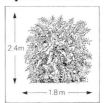

Suitable site and soil Most soils are suitable in a sunny or semi-shaded position where the plant can show itself off to full effect, especially as a large shrub.

Cultivation and care Plant out in autumn or winter. Prune after flowering, removing some old flowering stems. if you wish to keep its size down, cut back stems to non-flowering side growths after flowering.

AT A GLANCE

P. 'Belle Etoile'

P. coronarius 'Aureus'

Propagation Take softwood cuttings of young growth and root in sand in a frame in summer, or take longer, riper cuttings in autumn and root in a frame.

Recommended varieties The hybrids *P.* 'Beauclerk' and *P.* 'Belle Etoile' are both splendid, reliable shrubs; the former grows to 2.4m/8ft high and 1.8m/6ft wide, while the latter grows to 3m/10ft high by 3.6m/12ft wide. Both have fragrant, single white flowers in summer. *P.* 'Virginal' has pure white, strongly scented, double or semi-double flowers and grows to 3m/10ft by 1.5m/5ft. A good species for a dry, shady spot is *P. coronarius* which has creamy white flowers in early summer and grows to about 3m/10ft high; a good variety is *P.c.* 'Aureus' with yellow leaves. *P. microphyllus* is 90cm/3ft high with many sweetly scented flowers in summer.

Pests and diseases May suffer from aphids and leaf spot.

GOOD BASE
Philadelphus shrubs can benefit by underplanting with the hardy perennial *Astrantia major*, or the masterwort. This should be planted in large groups about 45cm/18in apart beneath the philadelphus shrubs.

PIERIS

Pieris 'Forest Flame'

These fully hardy evergreen shrubs are grown for their colourful and decorative foliage and for their small urn-shaped flowers, like lily-of-the valley, carried in sprays and drooping clusters.

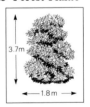

3.7m

1.8m

Suitable site and soil   Plant in a semi-shaded position in lime-free (acid) moist loam. Pick a sheltered site as the brilliant new foliage can be damaged by late frosts.

Cultivation and care   Plant out in early autumn or late spring. Prune if overgrown immediately after flowering by cutting back untidy shoots. Apply a top dressing of peat or leaf mould late in spring.

AT A GLANCE

SHADE TOLERANT

SHADE LOVING

LOVES DAMP SOIL

EVERGREEN

ACID SOIL ONLY

P. japonica 'Variegata'

P. formosa forrestii 'Wakehurst'

Propagation Increase by semi-ripe cuttings in summer.

Recommended varieties The hybrid *P.* 'Forest Flame' is a spectacular hardy shrub growing to 3.7m/12ft high by 1.8m/6ft wide. Its narrow, glossy leaves are red when young, changing to pink, to cream and then to dark green. It also has white flowers in spring. *P. floribunda* is a compact bushy shrub 1.8m/6ft high and wide with dark green glossy leaves. Its white flowers are borne in spring. *P. japonica* growing up to 3m/10ft has bronze-red young leaves which turn dark green. Good varieties are *P.j.* 'Blush', *P.j.* 'Scarlett O'Hara' and P.j. 'Variegata', a slow growing shrub with leaves edged in creamy-white. *P. formosa forrestii* 'Wakehurst', with brilliant red leaves in early summer, can grow 3m/10ft high by 4.6m/15ft wide or more in sheltered spots.

Pests and diseases Usually no problems.

BEST OF BOTH WORLDS

Some pieris produce their best flowers in sun but their best foliage in the shade. The dense shrub, *P. japonica* 'Blush', however, grows fine-quality flowers and foliage in light shade.

POLYGONATUM/*Solomon's seal*

Polygonatum × hybridum

This group of mostly hardy, herbaceous perennials is easy to grow and does well in shady borders (with a small one suitable for a rock garden). They are grown for their small clusters of delicate flowers.

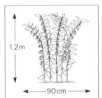

1.2 m

90 cm

Suitable site and soil Most do best in a well-drained, peaty soil in a shady and cool position in a border, perhaps under the shade of a taller border plant. *P. × hybridum* does well virtually anywhere as long as its roots are in shade. Plant *P. hookeri* in a shady spot in a rock garden.

Cultivation and care Plant in autumn or winter. They need very little attention and are happiest if left alone.

AT A GLANCE

SHADE TOLERANT

SHADE LOVING

GOOD FOR CUTTING

EASY TO GROW

PREFERS WELL-DRAINED SOIL

P. hookeri

P. commutatum

Propagation Increase by division at the planting time.

Recommended varieties *P.* × *hybridum* (Solomon's seal)
produces clusters of lovely green-tipped white flowers, borne
on arching stems that also bear long, light-green pointed
leaves. These plants grow to 1.2m/4ft high by 90cm/3ft wide
and should be planted about 45cm/1½ft apart. The shade-
loving, dwarf rock plant, *P. hookeri,* grows slowly to provide a
dense covering of small mid-green leaves which appear in late
spring and early summer at the same time as the spikes of
lilac-pink, small flowers about 2cm/½in long. The plant grows
to 5cm/2in high and spreads about 30cm/1ft. *P. commutatum*
(P. giganteum, giant Solomon's seal) grows up to 1.8m/6ft
high and does very well in fertile, moist soil.

Pests and diseases Usually no problems from diseases but
watch out for the caterpillars of the sawfly.

DELICATE DISPLAY
In late spring, the
flowers of the popular *P.*
× *hybridum*, borne on
arching stems, makes a
beautiful display as cut
flowers in a vase
alongside green foliage
of some sort. It is flower
arranging made easy.

POLYGONUM/*Russian vine, knotweed*

Polygonum baldschuanicum

This group contains hardy annuals, herbaceous perennials and deciduous climbers that are twining and woody-stemmed. Some are fully hardy and some only half hardy but all bear many tiny, bell-shaped flowers.

Suitable site and soil Most soils will do but herbaceous species prefer fertile, moist soil in sun or some shade. Young climbers do best if sheltered.

Cultivation and care Climbers should be planted out in early spring while herbaceous species should be planted out in autumn or winter. Support the young growth of climbers with twigs or sticks. Growth is vigorous so prune back hard.

AT A GLANCE

LOVES FULL SUN · SHADE TOLERANT · EASY TO GROW · PREFERS WELL-DRAINED SOIL · NEEDS PRUNING

P. baldschuanicum

P. bistorta 'Superbum'

Propagation Increase shrubby climbers by heel cuttings in summer or hardwood cuttings in mid autumn. Divide herbaceous species in early autumn or late winter.

Recommended varieties *P. baldschuanicum (P. aubertii* or *Fallopia baldschuanica*, Russian vine or mile-a-minute plant) is a hardy, fast-growing twining climber that can make 4.6m/ 15ft in a year; eventually it can grow to over 12m/40ft. It produces profuse pale pink or white flowers in clusters from midsummer to early autumn. *P. bistorta* 'Superbum' (snakeweed) is a herbaceous perennial border plant that grows up to 90cm/3ft and spreads to 60cm/2ft. It is vigorous and forms clumps or mats of light green, oval leaves and, in late spring/ early summer, produces spikes of pink flowers.

Pests and diseases Not usually prone to diseases but aphids may attack the climbers.

COVER UP
P. baldschuanicum (Russian vine) can cover up an ugly item or provide privacy in the garden. It quickly grows along wires or trellis and will produce thick growth year after year. It is not fussy about soil.

PULMONARIA/*lungwort*

Pulmonaria saccharata

Plants from this group of low growing, hardy perennials are grown for their ability to thrive in shade and their small appealing flowers in spring. They make good ground cover with interesting foliage.

Suitable site and soil Plant 30cm/12in apart in the front row of a shady border in any moist yet well-drained soil.

Cultivation and care Plant out in spring after flowering or in early autumn and be sure to keep the soil moist during the growing season.

Propagation Increase by division in spring or autumn.

AT A GLANCE

P. officinalis

P. angustifolia 'Munstead Blue'

Recommended varieties   Semi-evergreen *P. saccharata* flowers in early spring when the small funnel-shaped flowers open pink and then change to blue. It grows to 30cm/12in high by 60cm/2ft wide and has narrow, pointed and mottled leaves that make excellent ground cover. Another form, *P. s. argentea*, has silvery white leaves, while *P. s.* 'Pink Dawn' is grown for its small, pretty pink flowers. *P. officinalis* (common lungwort) has small, funnel-shaped, bluish-purple flowers produced in spring; it grows to 30cm/12in and has leaves similar to *P. saccharata*. *P. angustifolia* (blue cowslip) has plain leaves and bears small blue flowers in spring; a good variety is *P. a.* 'Munstead Blue'. *P. longifolia* grows to 30cm/12in and spreads to 45cm/18in and has very thin, dark green leaves. Its vivid blue flowers bloom in spring.

Pests and diseases   Usually few problems apart from mildew and sawfly larvae on leaves.

FRESH LEAVES
When the flowers of *P. saccharata* are over, the leaves tend to become tatty. So when flowering finishes, shear down to the base of the plant. A new crop soon appears and will look fresh for months.

PYRETHRUM

Pyrethrum roseum 'Brenda'

These hardy herbaceous perennials have attractive, daisy-like flowers on stiff stems, which make long-lasting cut flowers. They also have fine, ferny foliage. They are more properly part of the *Chrysanthemum* group.

Suitable site and soil Plant in light and well-drained soil in a sunny and open position in the middle of a medium-sized border.

Cultivation and care Plant out in early spring and stake for support. They need to be watered often while growing and when flowering has finished the stems should be cut back.

AT A GLANCE

LOVES FULL SUN

GOOD FOR CUTTING

PREFERS WELL-DRAINED SOIL

P. roseum mixed

P.roseum 'Eileen May Robinson'

Propagation Increase by division in late winter or after flowering. Can be grown from seed sown under glass in spring.

Recommended varieties There are many hybrids of *P. roseum (Chrysanthemum coccineum, Tanacetum coccineum)* with either single or double flowers. A good single-flowered variety is *P. r.* 'Brenda' which has fine, almost feathery foliage that is slightly scented. It grows to about 60cm/2ft high and spreads 45cm/18in, and produces attractive, daisy-like, magenta-pink flowers in late spring/early summer which are excellent for cutting. Another good single variety is the pink-flowered *P.r.* 'Eileen May Robinson'. Multi-coloured selections of *P.roseum* with mixtures of white, pink, rose red and crimson are available from seed suppliers in both double- and single-flowered forms.

Pests and diseases Usually no problems.

RAISED BEDS

Where the drainage is poor, these bright, daisy-like plants – which love light and well-drained soil – can be planted in raised beds or, alternatively, along the crest of a ridge or on a mound.

RHUS/*sumach*

Rhus typhina

Plants from this group of hardy
deciduous shrubs, small trees and
climbers are grown for their foliage –
especially their autumn colour – and
for their showy fruits. The sap of
some species is highly irritant to skin.

4.6m

6m

Suitable site and soil Put in an open sunny site in well-
drained, ordinary garden soil.

Cultivation and care Plant out between autumn and spring.
Requires little special care.

Propagation Increase by half-ripe cuttings in summer or by
planting suckers in the growing site in autumn.

AT A GLANCE

LOVES
FULL SUN

EASY
TO GROW

DECIDUOUS

PREFERS
WELL-
DRAINED
SOIL

R. hirta 'Laciniata'   *R. copallina*

Recommended varieties *R. typhina* (now more correctly *R. hirta*), the stag's horn sumach, is a large shrub that grows to 4.6m/15ft high and spreads to 6m/20ft. It gets its common name from the way its thick stems, covered in brown down, branch like antlers. The dense columns of greenish-white flowers form clusters of spherical fruits that are reddish-purple and velvet-textured. Its long leaves, made up of many segments, turn yellow, orange-red and crimson before they fall in the autumn. The leaves of *R. hirta* 'Laciniata' are more finely divided, rather like fern leaves. The upright shrub *R. copallina* (dwarf sumach) grows to about 1.2m/4ft high and wide and has many long, pointed leaflets that go purplish-red in autumn. Its small, yellow-green flowers borne in clusters in summer turn into oval, bright red fruits.

Pests and diseases Sometimes attacked by coral spot fungus.

ENCOURAGING FOLIAGE

It is unnecessary to prune *R. typhina* but you can encourage the vigorous shoots, on which its leaves grow, by cutting them down to ground level in late winter.

RIBES/*flowering currant*

R. sanguineum 'Pulborough Scarlet'

This group which contains evergreens and deciduous, hardy and half hardy flowering and fruiting shrubs includes the edible currants. In the ornamental garden, plants are mainly grown for their delicate flowers.

Suitable site and soil Most soils will do and a sunny or partially shaded site is preferred.

Cultivation and care Container-grown plants can be planted out at any time. Add compost or well-rotted manure as a top-dressing in spring and remove dead wood.

Propagation Propagate by cuttings in summer or autumn.

AT A GLANCE

LOVES FULL SUN

SHADE TOLERANT

EASY TO GROW

LOVES ALL SOIL

PREFERS WELL-DRAINED SOIL

R. speciosum

R. laurifolium

Recommended varieties The deciduous shrub *R. sanguineum* 'Pulborough Scarlet' is a hardy flowering currant that produces leaves early. It grows to a height and width of 2.4m/8ft and does well in town gardens, producing short hanging trails of bright, rose-coloured flowers in spring; the leaves are mildly aromatic and the flowers are followed by black fruits. Deciduous *R. alpinum* grows up 1.8m/6ft high by 1.2m/4ft wide and produces insignificant yellow-green flowers in spring, followed by round red berries. Deciduous, bushy and spiny, *R. speciosum* (fuchsia-flowered currant) grows to about 1.8m/6ft and has small, drooping, tubular red flowers, with long red stamens, in spring. *R. laurifolium* is a hardy evergreen growing to about 45cm/1½ft that does well in a rock garden. It has oval, leathery leaves and has yellow-green flowers in late winter.

Pests and diseases Watch out for aphids and leaf spot.

BETTERING YOUR HEDGES

R. alpinum makes a good hedge in poor soil and shade. Plant 38cm/15in apart and tip at 15cm/6in above the ground in summer, to encourage bushy growth. Shape annually.

ROBINIA/*false acacia, rose acacia*

Robinia pseudoacacia

This group of hardy and half-hardy flowering, deciduous trees and shrubs includes some popular ornamental specimen trees as well as others which are best trained against walls. All do well in poor soil and survive in dry areas.

12.5m

7.5m

Suitable site and soil A rather poor soil will do as long as it is well drained and the position is sunny with some shelter. Large trees should be given space in which to grow.

Cultivation and care Plant out during autumn and winter.

Propagation Increase by suckers; *R. pseudoacacia* can be grown from seed.

AT A GLANCE

LOVES
FULL SUN

LOVES
POOR
SOIL

DECIDUOUS

R. p. 'Frisia'

R. hispida

Recommended varieties The fast-growing *R. pseudoacacia* (false acacia) grows to 12.5m/20ft high and spreads 7.5m/25ft. It has dense, drooping clusters of fragrant, cream flowers in late spring and early summer and green oval leaflets. A good variety is *R. p.* 'Frisia' with beautiful and cheerful golden-yellow leaves which open in mid spring; they become pale green in midsummer. Another popular variety is *R. p.* 'Inermis' (mop-headed acacia) which lacks the spines of the other types and has a compact, mop-like form, but it seldom produces flowers. *R. kelseyi* grows to 2.4m/8ft and has deep pink flowers in early summer; its leaf stems are prickly. *R. hispida* (rose acacia) grows to 2.4m/8ft, producing hanging clusters of mid-pink flowers in early summer. Its dark green leaves are borne on bristly stems.

Pests and diseases Watch out for scale insects; otherwise there are usually no problems.

TREES AND TRAINING
R. kelseyi can be grown as a small standard tree as long as the suckers are removed and upright growth encouraged. *R. hispida's* vigorous shoots can be trained against a wall with twine.

ROSMARINUS/*rosemary*

Rosmarinus officinalis

This small group of evergreen flowering shrubs contains hardy and half-hardy species, which are grown in the border and rock garden for their flowers and aromatic foliage. The herb rosemary is one of the group.

Suitable site and soil   They do well in any well-drained, light garden soil in a sunny, yet sheltered site.

Cultivation and care   Plant out in spring. Very little special care is required except to tidy up plants by cutting out dead growth in late winter and cutting back overgrown shoots of *R. officinalis* at the same time.

AT A GLANCE

LOVES FULL SUN

FRAGRANT

EASY TO GROW

EVERGREEN

PREFERS WELL-DRAINED SOIL

R.o. 'Miss Jessopp's Upright' | R.o. prostratus

Propagation Increase from cuttings in summer.

Recommended varieties *R. officinalis* (rosemary) is a compact shrub that grows to 1.8m/6ft in height and spread. It is an attractive evergreen with long, narrow, dark green aromatic leaves that are whitish below and are used as a culinary herb. The small blue or mauve flowers appear in early spring and can continue until autumn. Two of the several varieties are the vigorous *R.o.* 'Miss Jessopp's Upright' and *R. o.* 'Benenden Blue' (or *R.o.* 'Collingwood Ingram'). *R.× lavandulaceus (R. officinalis prostratus)* is a low-growing, mat-forming shrub about 10cm/4in high and 1.2m/4ft across. It does well in sheltered rock gardens in a mild areas as it is not really hardy. Its leaves are a pale green and the small, pale blue flowers appear for most of the spring and summer.

Pests and diseases Usually no problems.

CUT AND DRIED

R. officinalis (rosemary) makes an excellent dried herb. Harvest it when the bush comes into flower in spring, then hang in small bunches in a warm, dark, dry place, where the air circulates freely, until brittle.

SALIX/*willow*

Salix 'Chrysocoma'

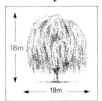

The deciduous, hardy trees and shrubs of this large group are grown for their shape and size, foliage and catkins. There are many willow types, from prostrate shrubs to large specimen trees.

Suitable site and soil A moist soil in a sunny site is best. The larger trees should not be planted in light sandy soils.

Cultivation and care Plant out in autumn or winter. In the right site, they will need little care, except, perhaps, to prune by removing dead wood between late autumn and late winter.

Propagation Increase by cuttings in autumn and winter.

AT A GLANCE

S. caprea pendula 'Kilmarnock'

S. lanata

Recommended varieties One of the best willows is the golden weeping willow, variously called *S.* 'Chrysocoma', *S. × sepulcralis chrysocoma* and *S. alba* 'Tristis'. It is a favourite specimen tree with shoots that almost reach to the ground. It can grow to 18m/60ft high and spreads about the same. *S. caprea* (pussy willow) is a shrub or tree that can grow to 9m/ 30ft high and spread 7.6m/25ft; its catkins emerge early in spring before its foliage. *S. repens argentea* (creeping willow) is a shrub with leaves covered in whitish downy hair and grey catkins in spring; in a dry soil, it reaches about 90cm/3ft high. *S. lanata* (woolly willow) is a bushy shrub that has woolly shoots and wide silvery leaves, produced with the greeny-yellow catkins in late spring. It grows to 75cm/2½ft high and spreads to 90cm/3ft.

Pests and diseases Watch out for leaf-eating and sap-sucking insects and for canker caused by fungal diseases.

WEEPING INTO THE WATER

A classic place to grow a really large willow is by a stretch of open, flowing water such as a stream or a small to medium-sized river. The weeping willows look especially good here.

Santolina/*cotton lavender*

Santolina chamaecyparissus

These hardy evergreen shrubs are grown for their unusual and delicately scented foliage and for their small, button-shaped flowers. There are varieties for the border and rock garden and for a low hedge.

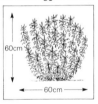

Suitable site and soil A sunny spot in well-drained soil.

Cultivation and care Plant out in early autumn or early spring. Cut back hard after flowering or in early spring so that the plants do not lose their shape. During summer, regularly trim hedging plants with shears.

Propagation Increase by cuttings taken in summer.

AT A GLANCE

LOVES FULL SUN

FRAGRANT

EVERGREEN

PREFERS WELL-DRAINED SOIL

S. neapolitana

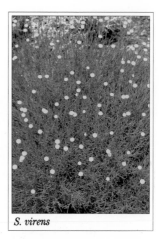

S. virens

Recommended varieties *S. chamaecyparissus* (cotton lavender or lavender cotton) is a rounded, evergreen shrub growing to 60cm/2ft high and wide. It has small, button-shaped yellow flowers in late summer but is grown primarily for its foliage; the shoots have a woolly protective coating, so that they appear to be almost white and the plant is densely covered with small, narrow, feather-like, aromatic leaves. It makes a good low hedge. *S. c. nana* is a dwarf form growing to about 38cm/15in. *S. pinnata neapolitana (S. neapolitana)*, which has a rounded bushy habit, also grows to about 75cm/2½ft high by 90cm/3ft wide and has pale yellow flowers carried on thin stems in summer; its foliage is dull green and feathery. *S. rosmarinifolia (S. virens)* has bright, thread-like green leaves and bright yellow flowers in midsummer; it grows to 60cm/2ft high and 90cm/3ft wide.

Pests and diseases Usually no problems.

BORDER COVER UP

Cotton lavender is a fine plant for the front of a mixed border. Its foliage is not only attractive but is also dense and can thus hide the otherwise unsightly stems of taller plants. Put the plants 45cm/18in apart.

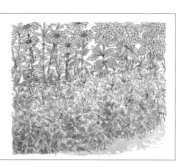

SCABIOSA/*scabious, pincushion flower*

Scabiosa caucasica

A few of this group of annuals and herbaceous perennials are grown in the garden for their daisy-like flowers which put on a bold display in beds and borders. They also make excellent, long-stemmed cut flowers.

Suitable site and soil   Plant in a sunny site where the soil is well-drained and preferably contains a little lime.

Cultivation and care   Plant perennials in early spring and cut old stems down in late autumn.

Propagation   Grow annuals from seed sown in the growing site in spring and perennials from seed in autumn. Perennials

AT A GLANCE

LOVES
FULL SUN

GOOD FOR
CUTTING

PREFERS
LIME

PREFERS
WELL-
DRAINED
SOIL

S. caucasica 'Miss Willmott'

S. atropurpurea

are also increased by cuttings taken in summer or by division early in spring.

Recommended varieties *S. caucasica* 'Clive Greaves' is a hardy perennial with attractive, 8cm/3in wide, blue-violet or mauve flowers on long stems appearing all summer long. It grows to about 60cm/2ft high and wide. Another good variety is *S. caucasica* 'Miss Willmott' which has white flowers. The annual *S. atropurpurea* (sweet scabious) is easy to grow from seed and the 'Sunburst' series is especially good. It grows to 90cm/3ft and spreads to 30cm/12in. *Scabiosa* Mixed Giant Hybrids (pincushion flower) in mixed colours with large flowers are easy to grow from seed. *S.* 'Butterfly Blue' has become a popular choice in recent years.

Pests and diseases Watch for signs of snails and slugs and powdery mildew. Root rot is caused when soil is too moist.

RUNNING TO SEED
These plants make excellent cut flowers. And if the flowers are allowed to form seed heads, these, when dried, can also be used in flower arrangements, to provide texture contrast in a vase.

SEMPERVIVUM/*houseleek*

Sempervivum tectorum

These hardy evergreen succulents are grown for their symmetrical rosettes of leaves, which gradually spread into wide masses, and for their star-shaped flowers. They are excellent in the rock garden.

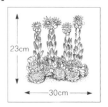

Suitable site and soil   Plant in a sunny position in a gritty and well-drained garden soil.

Cultivation and care   Plant out at any time except during summer. Once established, plants will look after themselves.

Propagation   Easily increased by replanting offsets in early autumn or early spring. Can also be grown from seed.

AT A GLANCE

LOVES
FULL SUN

EASY
TO GROW

EVERGREEN

PREFERS
WELL-
DRAINED
SOIL

S. arachnoideum

S. montanum

Recommended varieties   *S. tectorum* (common houseleek) is a tenacious and attractive hardy houseleek which grows to 8cm/3in and spreads to about 30cm/12in. Its leaf rosettes, shaped like a tongue with a spiked tip, are mid-green with reddish-purple tips. There are also forms with red leaves. It bears small purple flowers on 30cm/12in stems in summer. (A houseleek growing on a roof is said to be a sign of good luck.) *S. arachnoideum* (cobweb houseleek) has rosettes of red-tipped leaves covered with fine downy white hair. The plant grows up to 13cm/5in and spreads about 10cm/4in and produces red, star-shaped flowers in summer. *S. montanum* has fleshy green leaves and grows to about 15cm/6in by 10cm/4in. It produces clusters of dark red flowers in summer. *S.* 'Commander Hay' grows to 15cm/6in and spreads 30cm/12in. Its rosettes are a striking dark red.

Pests and diseases   Can be prone to rust and attack by vine weevil.

OFF THE WALL

Houseleeks can be grown in cracks and crevices in the smallest amounts of soil. They look especially good in a dry-stone wall. Spread about 2.5cm/1in of rich soil over it before planting.

Silene/*campion, catchfly*

Silene uniflora 'Flore Pleno'

Plants from this group of annuals and herbaceous perennials are grown for their attractive flowers produced all summer long. They put on a charming display in the rock garden or border or as a bedding plant.

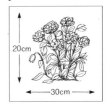

Suitable site and soil   Most well-drained soils suit these plants which do best in full sun or partial shade.

Cultivation and care   Plant perennials in autumn or winter.

Propagation   Annuals can be grown from seed sown on the flowering site. Some perennials are easily grown from seed. Perennials are also grown from cuttings taken in spring.

AT A GLANCE

S. acaulis

S. schafta

Recommended varieties   Perennial *S. uniflora* 'Flore Pleno'
(*S. vulgaris maritima* 'Flore Pleno', sea campion) grows to
about 20cm/8in and spreads about 30cm/12in, with grey-green
leaves and double white flowers in summer. The evergreen
S.acaulis (moss campion) has small vivid green leaves that
form a mat-like growth; in spring, it bears a mass of small pink
flowers. *S. armeria* (sweet William catchfly), an annual that
grows to about 38cm/15in and spreads 15cm/6in, is easily
grown from seed and produces greyish foliage and clusters of
bright pink or red flowers through most of the summer. *S.
pendula* 'Triumph' is a showy annual with soft, hairy leaves
and graceful, drooping sprays of double red flowers in summer.
It grows to 23cm/9in and spreads 15cm/6in. *S.schafta* is an
easily grown perennial which has deep pink flowers in summer
and autumn.

Pests and diseases   Usually no problems.

BLOOMING STONES

S. armeria is such an
easy plant to grow from
seed that it can be sown
almost anywhere, then
virtually ignored. Scatter
seed on an old wall or
pile of stones for
summer-long, bright
pink and red flowers.

SORBUS/*rowan, mountain ash, whitebeam*

Sorbus aria 'Lutescens'

These hardy deciduous trees and shrubs are grown for their flowers, leaf shape, autumn colour and attractive berries. Many are sturdy plants that do well in shade and in towns where air quality is poor.

Suitable site and soil   A well-drained, but not too dry, soil in sun or partial shade is best. They tolerate some lime.

Cultivation and care   Plant out in autumn or winter. If a plant grows too large, it can be thinned in autumn or winter.

Propagation   Can be grown from seed in autumn, by cuttings in summer or by grafting in winter.

AT A GLANCE

S. aucuparia

S. 'Joseph Rock'

Recommended varieties   *S. aria* 'Lutescens' (whitebeam) is
a delightful small tree that can grow to about 8m/26ft high and
spread 7m/23ft. Its young foliage is silvery grey, becoming
greener later. In late spring and early summer, it produces
clusters of white flowers followed by orange-red berries in
autumn. *S. aucuparia* (mountain ash, rowan) is a neat tree
usually between 6m/20ft to 15m/50ft high by half as much
wide; its leaves turn yellow, then orange in autumn. It has
clusters of creamy white flowers in summer and orange-yellow
fruits in autumn. *S.* 'Joseph Rock' is an upright tree that grows
to about 7.5m/25ft high. Its bright green leaves take on vibrant
hues of purple, red and orange in autumn. The white flowers
in late spring are followed by yellow berries in autumn.

Pests and diseases   There are usually no problems with
pests but trees and shrubs may be attacked by fireblight in
mild areas.

FEED THE BIRDS

S. aucuparia attracts a
diverse range of grateful,
hungry birds. If planted
where it can be seen
from a window, it
provides a continuous
display of birds in
autumn that will feast off
its copious fruits.

SPIRAEA/*bridal wreath, foam of May*

Spirea 'Arguta'

These hardy, deciduous shrubs contain some attractive garden varieties. They can be used as specimen shrubs, in a border or as hedging. Mostly grown for their flowers, some also have interesting foliage.

Suitable site and soil   An open sunny site is best in a deep, fertile soil that is well-drained but not too dry.

Cultivation and care   Plant out in autumn or winter. Established hedges need a trim every year. All types need attention after flowering, when they should be thinned out.

Propagation   Increase by cuttings in summer.

AT A GLANCE

S. japonica

S. japonica 'Little Princess'

Recommended varieties *S.* 'Arguta' (*S.* × *arguta;* bridal wreath, foam of May), which grows to 2.1m/7ft high and wide, produces profuse cascades of flowers in mid to late spring when its arching branches are densely covered in clusters of small white flowers. These are followed by small fresh green leaves which turn a subtle red in autumn. *S. japonica* (syn. *S.* × *bumalda*) 'Little Princess' has pink flowers in mid and late summer. A low-growing, mound-forming shrub, it grows to about 90cm/3ft and spreads about 1.5m/5ft. All varieties of *S. japonica* do best if pruned hard in late winter. Vigorous *S. douglasii* grows to 1.8m/6ft and produces long, dense clusters of purplish-pink flowers in summer. Its pendulous branches are densely covered in grey-green leaves that are downy underneath. This shrub can be increased by division.

Pests and diseases Usually no problems but leaves may be attacked by sawfly.

SPRING DISPLAY

Plant tall, pretty tulips in front of *S.* 'Arguta', so that the bridal wreath flowers cascade on to the tulip blooms. When the tulips have finished, take them out and put in summer bedding plants.

SYMPHORICARPOS/*snowberry, coralberry, Indian currant*

Symphoricarpos albus laevigatus

Grown for their berries, this group of hardy, deciduous shrubs provides interest through the winter and makes excellent ground cover as well as good hedging. There is a range of berry colours.

Suitable site and soil   Will grow almost anywhere in sun or shade in almost any type of well-drained soil.

Cultivation and care   Plant out from mid autumn through winter; once established, they look after themselves. Hedges need regular trimming and overgrown plants should be thinned out between mid autumn and mid winter. Remove suckers occasionally or the plant will take over the garden.

AT A GLANCE

LOVES FULL SUN   SHADE TOLERANT   NEEDS PRUNING   EASY TO GROW   DECIDUOUS   PREFERS WELL-DRAINED SOIL

S. orbiculatus 'Foliis Variegatis'   *S.* × *chenaultii* 'Hancock'

Propagation   The easiest way is to put rooted suckers in the growing site from mid autumn to mid winter.

Recommended varieties   *S. albus laevigatus* (snowberry) grows to about 1.8m/6ft high and spreads about 2.1m/7ft. It is a sturdy shrub with dense foliage and dark green leaves. Its small pink flowers produced in summer are followed in autumn by white round fruits which last from autumn right through winter. A good variety of *S. orbiculatus* (coralberry, Indian currant) is *S.o.* 'Foliis Variegatis' which is a compact bushy shrub that grows to about 1.2m/4ft and spreads about 1.8m/6ft. It has small green leaves edged with yellow and in mid and late summer small pink flowers in short clusters. *S.* × *chenaultii* 'Hancock' makes excellent ground cover.

Pests and diseases   May suffer from leaf spot.

WINTER ARRANGEMENT

The large white fruits of *S. albus laevigatus* can be used in indoor displays in autumn or winter. They look good on their own but they can be combined with some evergreen foliage.

Taxus baccata

This group of evergreen conifers contains some familiar trees, many of which are almost indestructibly hardy. They are grown as specimen trees, as hedges and for topiary. Most parts of the yew are poisonous.

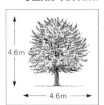

Suitable site and soil   Almost any soil – acid or alkaline – will do for yew as long as it is not waterlogged. They do well in sun or shade.

Cultivation and care   Plant out between mid autumn and early spring. If you want to shape a yew, prune it hard in late spring. Yews can also be lightly trimmed all summer. Yews are drought resistant.

AT A GLANCE

T.b. 'Dovastonii Aurea'

T.b. 'Fastigiata'

Propagation   *T. baccata* can be grown from seed but other selected forms must be propagated by cuttings in summer or autumn.

Recommended varieties   The familiar *T.baccata* (common yew) can eventually grow large, but expect a height and spread of about 4.6m/15ft after 20 years. It has reddish scaly bark, with branches spread horizontally; the leaves are needle-like and dark green. If left to grow unchecked, it will become broadly pyramid-shaped and older trees have dome-shaped crowns. *T.b.* 'Dovastonii Aurea' has yellow-edged leaves and golden shoots; it grows to about 7.6m/25ft high and 6m/20ft across. *T.b.* 'Fastigiata' (Irish yew) is erect and column-like and usually reaches a height of about 7.5m/25ft.

Pests and diseases   Watch out for mites, scale insects and gall midge larvae.

ANY SHAPE YEW CHOOSE

T. baccata is often used by topiarists. Work should start when a yew is about 1.5m/5ft tall. Once the basic topiary form has been attained, strict annual clipping keeps it in shape.

THYMUS/*thyme, lemon thyme*

Thymus vulgaris

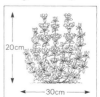

These hardy and half-hardy herbaceous perennials and sub-shrubs are grown for their herbal properties – all have aromatic leaves – and as decorative plants and ground cover in the rock garden.

Suitable site and soil   A sunny, open site in a well-drained soil will do. Mat-forming types look good in gaps in paving.

Cultivation and care   Plant out from mid autumn to late winter. Give a light trim to remove old flower heads after flowering and replace plants every few years, as they tend to die from the centre. Harvest thyme for drying when it begins to flower, taking non-flowering shoots.

AT A GLANCE

LOVES FULL SUN

FRAGRANT

EVERGREEN

PREFERS WELL-DRAINED SOIL

T.v. aureus

T. × citriodorus

Propagation   Mat-forming types can be increased by division at almost any time. Upright or bushy types can be increased by cuttings in early summer.

Recommended varieties   *T. vulgaris* (common thyme) is one of the most important garden herbs and it produces aromatic, dark green leaves. It can grow to 20cm/8in and spreads about 30cm/12in, producing clusters of small mauve flowers in early summer. The variety *T. v. aureus* has yellow leaves and is also suitable for culinary use. *T. × citriodorus* (lemon thyme) grows to about 30cm/12in high and wide and has delightful lemon-scented leaves. Good in the rock garden is *T. herbabarona*, growing to 13cm/5in high by 38cm/15in wide, which forms an aromatic mat smelling of caraway; it also has clusters of small lilac flowers in early summer.

Pests and diseases   Usually no problems, except for leaf roller caterpillars.

THYME FOR A BATH

Lemon thyme *(T. × citriodorus)* is a good skin tonic. One easy way to use it is to put the leaves into a muslin (cheesecloth) bag which can be added to bathwater for a refreshing, soothing soak.

TRADESCANTIA/*spiderwort, trinity flower, wandering jew*

Tradescantia × *andersoniana* 'Osprey'

This group of perennials contains some well-loved, tender varieties grown in the greenhouse and as house-plants and some hardy varieties for herbaceous borders. They are grown for their foliage and flowers.

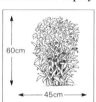

60cm

45cm

Suitable site and soil Hardy varieties do best in well-drained soil in sun. Put greenhouse varieties in a good potting compost in a bright spot out of direct sun.

Cultivation and care Plant out hardy varieties in autumn or winter and cut down in mid to late autumn. Greenhouse varieties should be watered sparingly and kept above 10°C/5°F in winter; water plants freely during the growing period

AT A GLANCE

SHADE TOLERANT

EASY TO GROW

PREFERS WELL-DRAINED SOIL

T. × a. 'Isis'

T. fluminensis 'Variegata'

and feed with a dilute liquid fertilizer every 14 days.

Propagation Hardy varieties can be divided in early spring while greenhouse varieties should be increased by tip cuttings in spring and summer.

Recommended varieties A good variety of *T. × andersoniana (T. virginiana;* spiderwort, trinity flower), a hardy herbaceous perennial, is *T. × a.* 'Osprey'. It grows to 60cm/2ft high and spreads 45cm/18in and has delightful white flowers with blue centres produced all summer long. Similar is *T. ×. a.* 'Isis' with purple flowers. A familiar house-plant and greenhouse plant is trailing *T. fluminensis* 'Variegata' (wandering jew) with oval leaves, which turn purple underneath in bright sun, on short stalks.

Pests and diseases   Usually no problems apart from slugs.

ON THE TRAIL
Robust and fast-growing, *T. fluminensis* 'Quicksilver' is an interesting trailing variety, which tends to keep its basal leaves longer than others, and is thus ideal in a hanging basket in a warm conservatory.

VERONICA/*speedwell*

Veronica gentianoides

This group contains hardy and frost-hardy herbaceous perennials grown for their attractive, usually blue flowers. Taller varieties are found in the border and the dwarf ones look good in the rock garden.

Suitable site and soil Plant rock garden types in ordinary well-drained soil in a sunny site and border types in rich, well-drained soil in sun or in partial shade.

Cultivation and care Plant out between autumn and spring. Tall varieties might need support in windy sites; cut down border herbaceous perennials in mid autumn. Where the soil tends to dry out, water border varieties in dry spells.

AT A GLANCE

LOVES
FULL SUN

SHADE
TOLERANT

EASY
TO GROW

PREFERS
WELL-
DRAINED
SOIL

V. longifolia

V. prostrata

Propagation Increase by division in early spring; rock garden types can also be propagated from cuttings in summer.

Recommended varieties *V. gentianoides*, the fully hardy border perennial, has glossy, light green leaves and grows to about 45cm/18in high and wide. It bears slender, pale blue flower spikes on stems in early summer. Also for the border, *V. longifolia* grows to 1.2m/4ft and spreads about 30cm/12in and has pointed, mid-green leaves; it produces spikes of deep blue flowers for most of the summer. *V. prostrata* is a good rock garden, mat-forming plant that grows to only 8cm/3in but spreads 45cm/18in, with deep blue flowers from early to mid summer. *V. filiformis* is another mat-forming plant that grows to 5cm/2in but spreads rapidly to 90cm/3ft. It has bright blue flowers in spring and early summer.

Pests and diseases Powdery mildew may attack leaves.

COVER UP
V. filiformis is an excellent plant for quickly covering up a bare mound in a rock garden. It grows in sun and shade and needs to be controlled after a year or so or it will become troublesome.

VIBURNUM

Viburnum × burkwoodii

This group contains evergreen and deciduous hardy shrubs. Some varieties flower in winter when the shrub is otherwise bare and others flower in spring and summer. Several varieties have fragrant blooms.

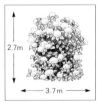

2.7m

3.7m

Suitable site and soil Plant in moist, rich soil in a sunny sheltered spot protected from morning sun in winter.

Cultivation and care Plant out during autumn or winter. Thin out or remove dead or old wood after flowering.

Propagation Take cuttings in early to mid summer or in late summer. Alternatively, try layering or growing from seed.

AT A GLANCE

LOVES
FULL SUN

DECIDUOUS

EVERGREEN

V. farreri

V. opulus 'Compactum'

Recommended varieties *V.* × *burkwoodii* is a favourite semi-evergreen spreading shrub with large heads of small flowers produced from early to late spring; these flowers form pink buds, then white flowers and have a heady fragrance. It grows to about 2.7m/9ft and can spread 3.7m/12ft. *V. farreri* (syn. *V. fragrans*), growing to about 2.7m/9ft height and spread, is a deciduous, winter-flowering shrub with leaves that are bronze when young. Deciduous, more spreading, *V. plicatum* 'Marie-sii' has white flowers in spring and reddish leaves in autumn. Evergreen *V. tinus* grows 2.1m/7ft by 2.1m/7ft, with white flowers from mid autumn to late spring. Deciduous *V. opulus* 'Compactum' grows to 1.8m/6ft and has red berries in autumn.

Pests and diseases Aphids can infest the leaves and grey mould can be a problem on dead shoots. The leaves are prone to spotting from fungal infections.

SPECIMEN CHOICE
If you have a small garden, choose *V. carlesii* 'Aurora' which grows to about 1.2m/4ft high and wide. With more space, try *V. plicatum* 'Mariesii' which reaches 3m/10ft high by 4.6m/15ft wide.

VIOLA/*violet, pansy*

Viola × wittrockiana

All the violas commonly grown are hardy perennials, but pansies are generally treated as half-hardy annuals or as hardy biennials. Most violas are grown for their flowers, but the sweet violet is grown for fragrance.

23cm

20cm

Suitable site and soil Moist yet well-drained soils in sun or partial shade suit most plants in this group.

Cultivation and care Plant in early autumn or early spring. Remove dead blooms to prolong flowering.

Propagation Many pansies and violas are grown from seed sown in a frame or the garden in summer, but those used for

AT A GLANCE

LOVES FULL SUN

SHADE TOLERANT

EASY TO GROW

LOVES DAMP SOIL

PREFERS WELL-DRAINED SOIL

V. cornuta 'Alba'

V. odorata

summer bedding are often sown under glass in late winter. All species can also be propagated from basal shoot cuttings.

Recommended varieties   *V. × wittrockiana* (pansy) are the showy hybrids that grow to 23cm/9in high and spread 20cm/8in. Most flower from winter through to early summer. *V. cornuta* 'Alba' (horned violet) is excellent in the rock garden or at the bed edge. It grows to 23cm/9in high by 30cm/12in wide and has blue, purple or white flowers in early summer. *V. labradorica* 'Purpurea', 13cm/5in high by a spread of about 30cm/12in, will spread by seeding and has mauve flowers in late spring with the leaves tinged with purple, where exposed to the sun. *V. odorata* (sweet violet) has small, scented blue or white flowers in spring (height 10cm/4in; spread 23cm/9in).

Pests and diseases   Prone to several types of fungal infection including those causing leaf spot and rust.

WEED CONTROL
V. cornuta (horned violet), with its delicate five-petalled flowers in early summer, is good at keeping down weeds. Plant 30cm/12in apart and it quickly covers a bed.

WEIGELA

Weigela florida

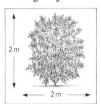

In late spring and summer, these fully hardy deciduous shrubs put on a colourful display of small flowers. A couple of species are commonly cultivated in the garden, along with a number of hybrid varieties.

Suitable site and soil Plant in a position where there is either full sun or partial shade and in a fertile, well-drained soil that remains moist even in dry weather.

Cultivation and care Plant out from early autumn to late winter. Water if the soil is drying out completely. Prune immediately after flowering is over by shortening spent shoots. At other times, remove older branches to keep vigorous.

AT A GLANCE

LOVES FULL SUN

SHADE TOLERANT

NEEDS PRUNING

DECIDUOUS

PREFERS WELL-DRAINED SOIL

W. florida 'Foliis Purpureis'

W. 'Bristol Ruby'

Propagation Increase by softwood cuttings taken in summer.

Recommended varieties *W. florida* is an excellent species often represented by the compact form *W.f.* 'Foliis Purpureis' which has funnel-shaped flowers that are strongly pink on the outside and light pink inside. Its leaves have a purple tinge and it grows to about 90cm/3ft high and 1.5m/5ft wide. Another good species is *W. middendorffiana* which grows and spreads to 1.2m/4ft, with bright yellow flowers borne in late spring. The hybrid *W.* 'Bristol Ruby' has rich red flowers in late spring and in early summer and grows to 2.4m/8ft and spreads 1.8m/6ft. Its leaves are mid green. *W.* 'Looymansii Aurea' grows to 1.5m/5ft and has yellowish foliage and pale pink flowers. It should be shielded from hot sun. *W.* 'Candida' has white flowers which appear in late spring and early summer.

Pests and diseases Usually no problems.

PROPER PRUNING
When a plant has become old and untidy, it could be time to cut about half of it right back to the trunk in spring, losing this year's flowering but ensuring better blooms next year.

ZANTEDESCHIA/*arum lily, calla*

Zantedeschia aethiopica 'Crowborough'

Popular for the greenhouse, as houseplants and for occasional outdoor cultivation, these perennial, rhizomatous half-hardy and tender plants are grown for their spectacular flowers.

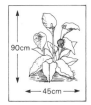

Suitable site and soil   In the greenhouse, plant in a 25cm/10in pot in a suitable potting compost. Outdoors in mild areas plant *Z. aethiopica* in sun or partial shade in moisture retentive soil or in boggy ground near a pond.

Cultivation and care   In a greenhouse, plant in late winter. Water freely during growing period and after flowering reduce watering until dry, then store until late winter.

AT A GLANCE

LOVES
FULL SUN

Z. elliottiana

Z. rehmannii

Propagation Increase by separating offsets in winter.

Recommended varieties   The variety of *Z. aethiopica* (arum lily, calla) *Z.a.* 'Crowborough' may survive outdoors in mild areas. It grows up to 90cm/3ft and spreads 45cm/18in and in spring and early summer produces its 'flowers', each with a white spathe and a central, perky, erect yellow spadix. The leaves, produced around the base of the plant, are large and deep green. Tender *Z. elliottiana* (golden arum lily, golden calla) grows to 60cm/2ft high and and spreads 60cm/2ft and has green leaves spotted with white. It produces bright yellow spathes and spadixes. Tender *Z. rehmannii* (pink arum lily, pink calla) grows about 30cm/12in high and wide and had pink to red spathes and yellow spadixes.

Pests and diseases Watch out for cucumber mosaic virus and tomato-spotted wilt virus.

ARUM BY THE WATER

Z. aethiopica's blooms make a striking display in spring and summer when grown in shallow water at the margins of a pond. Plant in a plastic basket filled with soil in about 23cm/9in of water.

GLOSSARY OF GARDEN TERMS

alpine A plant that grows naturally in the Alps; usually refers to plants suitable for rockeries, as these plants have a dwarf, compact habit.

annual A plant that germinates from seed, grows, flowers, sets seeds and dies within a year.

aquatic A plant adapted to living in water.

bed A clearly defined plot within a garden.

bedding plant Any plant that is used as part of a temporary garden display.

biennial A plant that completes its life cycle in two years (and dies after flowering in the second season).

bog garden A permanently wet, artificial garden, usually sited alongside a stream or water garden.

border A cultivated area running alongside a path, wall or boundary fence.

bud The growing point of a shoot.

burr A seed head, flower case or fruit with bristles or spines.

bush A low shrub whose branches all grow from ground level.

chipping Nicking the outer coating of a seed, to speed up germination.

climber A plant that ascends towards the light.

cloche A moveable cover made from plastic or glass used for protecting early crops.

cold frame A small, unheated permanent structure with a glass roof where seedlings can be hardened off.

compost There are two types: the first is 'garden' compost, made from decomposed vegetable waste, grass clippings and other bio-degradable refuse; the second is a mixture of loam, peat and sand, used for potting.

conifer Generally an evergreen tree or shrub that has needles and bears seeds in cones.

crown The part of a herbaceous plant from which the roots grow down and the stem grows up.

cultivar A cultivated variety of a plant; it differs from a naturally occuring variety.

dead-heading Picking off dead flower heads to tidy plants and encourage further flowering.

deciduous Refers to a tree or shrub which sheds its leaves in autumn or winter.

dibber A hand tool for making holes in soil.

dormant	The inactive period, during winter, when a plant's growth temporarily ceases.
drill	An outdoor furrow in which seeds are sown.
dwarf	A miniature form of a plant.
evergreen	Refers to a tree or shrub which keeps its leaves throughout the year.
fertilizer	A substance that supplies nutrients to soil.
floret	An individual flower that forms part of a larger flower head.
genus	A group of closely related plant species.
germination	The sprouting of a seed.
grafting	Joining a shoot or cutting from one plant to the stem of another, to form a new plant.
ground cover	A carpet of low-growing, often spreading plants.
half-hardy	Plants that cannot withstand heavy frost.
hardening off	Allowing tender and half-hardy plants that have been raised under glass to get used to outdoor conditions.
hardy	Plants that are able to withstand frosts; they can survive outdoors all year round in all but the most severe weather conditions.
herbaceous	Plants that produce soft, non-woody growth; they die down in winter, after seeding, and reappear in the spring.
humidity	The amount of water vapour in the atmosphere.
humus	Organic constituent of soil.
hybrid	A plant derived from crossing two varieties, usually of the same species or genus.
insecticide	Any substance, including chemical compounds, that will destroy garden pests.
invasive	Refers to plants which tend to spread too vigorously if not kept in check.
leaf-mould	A compost made from decayed leaves, that increases soil fertility.
loam	A rich soil consisting of clay, sand and decayed vegetable matter.
mulch	A layer of organic material or plastic spread on the soil's surface, around plants, to discourage weeds and preserve moisture in the soil.
nitrogen	The most essential element in plant nutrition.
organic	Produced without artificial chemicals.
oxygenator	Aquatic plant that releases oxygen through its leaves.
peat	Partially decomposed vegetable matter that retains moisture.

perennial	A plant that lives for more than two years.
pergola	A canopy or covered walk formed by plants trained over a series of arches.
perpetual	Flowering plants that produce blooms intermittently throughout the year.
pinching	Removing tips of unwanted growing shoots using finger and thumb.
pricking out	Re-planting seedlings into beds or larger containers.
propagation	Increasing plants from seeds or cuttings or by grafting, budding, division or layering.
pruning	The controlled cutting back of branches to promote growth, encourage flowers and fruit, restrict size, or shape the plant.
screen	A wall, fence or hedge that encloses a garden or obscures an unattractive view.
seed leaf	First leaf or pair of leaves produced by a germinating seed.
seedling	A young plant, usually raised from seed, with a single, unbranched stem.
semi-evergreen	Refers to shrubs or trees which lose a proportion of their leaves in winter or early spring.
shrub	A woody plant, smaller than a tree, with stems that grow from near ground level and no central trunk.
species	A class of plants that have common characteristics and that breed consistently true to type from seed.
specimen plant	Any plant that is grown to create an effect when viewed from different angles.
succulent	A plant adapted to dry conditions, that has fleshy leaves and stems that store moisture.
tap root	A long, anchoring root that grows vertically downwards.
tender	Plants that are liable to damage from frost.
topiary	The art of training and clipping trees and shrubs into shapes.
tree	A plant with a central woody main stem or trunk.
variegated	Describes a leaf or petal marked with two or more distinct colours.
variety	A variant of a species arising naturally or through cultivation.
weed	Any plant that grows where it is not wanted, particularly when it competes with cultivated plants for light, moisture or food, or when it encourages pests and diseases.

INDEX

ACKNOWLEDGEMENTS

The publishers extend their
thanks to the following
agencies, companies and
individuals who have
kindly provided illustrative
material for this book. The
alphabetical name of the
supplier is followed by the
page and position of the
picture/s.

Abbreviations: b = bottom,
l = left, r = right, t = top.

Gillian Beckett: 8tl, 20tl, 41,
52tr, 58tl & tr, 60tr; Pat
Brindley: 8tr, 10tl & tr, 32tr,
33, 44tl, 49, 51; Brian
Carter/The Garden Picture
Library: 22tr, 27;
Collections/Patrick Johns:
34tr; Eric Crichton: 7, 9, 15,
24tl, 37, 38tl & tr, 43, 48tl,
50tl, 55, 57, 129; The Garden
Picture Library: 40tl; John
Glover: 16tr, 42tl; John
Glover/The Garden Picture
Library: 64tr; Derek Gould:
24tr, 25, 56tl & tr; Neil
Holmes: 44tr, 60tl; Photos
Horticultural: 12tr, 20tr, 21,
23, 28tr, 29, 30tl & tr, 39,
46tr, 47, 52tl, 54tl & tr, 59,
61, 62tr, 63, 67, 71, 75, 76tl &
tr, 78tl, 80tl, 83, 84tl, tr, 85,
86tl & tr, 87, 88tl & tr, 90tl,
92tl, 97, 98tl, 100tl & tr,
102tl, 103, 104tr, 106tr, 107,
111, 112tl, 112, 115, 116tl, 117,
118tr, 119 & back cover, 121,
122tr, 124tr, 125, 126tr, 127,
128tl, 130tl, 131, 133, 134tl &
tr, 136tl & tr, 138tl, 139,
140tr, 141, 144tl & tr, 145,
146tl & tr, 147, 148tr, 150tl,
152tr, 154tl, 155, 156tr, 158tl
& tr, 160tl, 162tl & tr, 164tr,
165, 167, 168tl & tr, 170tl,
171, 172tl & tr, 173, 176tl &
tr, 178tl & tr, 179, 180tl & tr,
182tr, 183, 184tl & tr, 186tl &
tr; Andrew Lawson: 13, 14tl,
16tl, 32tl; MC Picture
Library: front cover (Colin
Watmough), 14tr, 17, 18tl &
tr, 53, 65, 66tl, 70tl & tr, 73 &
title page, 74tl & tr, 81, 82tl,
94tl & tr, 109, 114tl & tr,
118tl; Peter McHoy: 26tl;
Tania Midgely: 42tr; David
Russell/The Garden Picture
Library: 22tl; Harry Smith
Collection: 11, 12tl, 19, 26tr,
28tl, 31, 34tl, 35, 36tl & tr,
40tr, 45, 46tl, 48tr, 50tr, 62tl,
64tl, 66tr, 68tl & tr, 69, 72tl &
tr, 77, 78tr, 79, 80tr, 82tr, 89,
90tr, 91, 92tr, 93, 95, 96tl &
tr, 97, 98, 99 & back cover,
101, 102tr, 104tl, 105, 106tl,
108tl & tr, 110tl & tr, 112tr,
116tr, 120tl & tr, 122tl, 123,
124tl, 126tl, 128tr, 130tr, 132tl
& tr, 135, 137, 138tr, 140tl,
142tl & tr, 143, 148tl, 149,
150tr, 151, 152tl, 154tr,
156tl, 157, 159, 160tr, 161,
163, 164tl, 166tl & tr, 169,
170tr, 174tl & tr, 175, 177,
181, 182tl, 185.